THE ROMANY WAY

Cover: A young Romany mother and son at their summer camp near Weymouth;
Overleaf: the author (right) chatting with gypsies in their camp, Wiltshire.

The Romany
Way

Irene Soper

EX LIBRIS PRESS

Published in 1994;
reprinted in 1996 by
EX LIBRIS PRESS
1 The Shambles
Bradford on Avon
Wiltshire
BA15 1JS

Typeset in 11 point Century Schoolbook

Design and typesetting by Ex Libris Press

Cover printed by Shires Press, Trowbridge
Printed and bound in Britain by
Cromwell Press Ltd., Broughton Gifford, Wiltshire

ISBN 0 948578 65 3

Acknowledgements: To Faber & Faber for extracts from
The Herbal Handbook by Juliette de Bairacli Levy; to Juliette
de Bairacli Levy for extract from her book, *Wanderers in the
New Forest*.

CONTENTS

Introduction

THE TRUE ROMANIES, WHOSE ORIGINS are in the far away land of India, are a mysterious and fascinating race. With their swarthy skin, dark hair, and quick speech they are unique. Travelling across Europe from their native land they brought with them the ancient and sacred language of India. Although Romany is no longer a spoken language there are many phrases and a large vocabulary still used.

It is said there are some three thousand words, the greater part of which are of Indian origin being connected with Sanskrit, whilst the rest consists of words from various languages picked up by the Gypsies in their wanderings from the East.

How refreshing it is to listen to their own unmistakable dialect sprinkled here and there with those lovely words from their own language, words like *mulleno* meaning haunted *naome* butchers broom and *aladge* ashamed.

These travellers cannot stay long at any one place as they have to be on the move to provide keep for their horses. Although constantly travelling they find time to practise their talents and skills such as carving and decorating their vans, peg-making and basket-weaving.

The Gypsies, as these travelling folk are commonly called, are hardy and enduring, living as they do with the elements throughout the seasons. It is a hard life with a strenuous routine which has to be followed each day regardless of the weather. Water is essential and sometimes they have to travel miles to fetch it, not only for themselves but for their horses also. Firewood is another necessity which has to be gathered and dried. Whether they cook outside over the camp-fire or on the small stoves in their vans, wood is the only fuel available to them.

Over the last fifteen years most of the travellers have been forced to live in special compounds and some even in houses. They had little choice as they were being constantly moved on and many of their regular stopping places were fenced off or the entrances blocked. Now, happily, more Romany families are again taking to the road to seek out the old droves and wide grass verges on which to camp along the way.

These families are descendants of the old English tribes – Lees, Coopers, Peters, Kings, Turners, Sheens – and many others. They are now beginning to appreciate the values of their Romany origins as more and more they become aware of their special cultures. Their gifts of prophecy, music and healing and the affinity they have with horses make them a race to be envied.

The Gypsy women need little if any make-up to enhance their natural beauty. The only adornments to their beautifully sculpted features are the golden earrings so loved by them. These are as traditional to the Gypsy women as the neck-scarf *or dicklo* is the Gypsy man.

It is these real travelling folk that this book is about.

Travelling Folk

It was New Year's Day and a bitter wind was blowing across the Wiltshire downs. As I motored along the open road I saw what I thought to be the green canvas roofs of three bow-top vans nestling in the shelter of bushes along a drove. Surely Gypsies living in this way was a thing of the past. However, on reaching the top of the hill, I saw a Gypsy boy come out of the wood dragging a dead branch and walk toward the vans.

Hastily parking the car I approached the camp, rather apprehensively, on foot. There were bantams running around and a black and white collie dog which was tied to one of the vans barked loudly. The biting easterly wind channelled down the fold in the hills and gusted on to the drove where the Romany family were sitting around a camp fire. Over the flames a cauldron filled with water was steaming, and close by in the grass was a large black kettle. Scattered about the ground were cooking utensils and another kettle. The nearby bushes were decorated with washing and bundles of long bramble stems were neatly tied up and stacked against a tree.

The Gypsy man was wearing a trilby hat and was colourfully dressed in a red plaid shirt with a pink silk scarf loosely knotted around his neck. Looking at the woman there was no doubt as to her Romany origins. The mauve jumper which she wore enhanced her olive skin, and her long dark hair which was parted in the middle was drawn back into a plait showing her golden-hooped ear-rings. Her dark eyes twinkled as she spoke with the quick staccato dialect which is characteristic of a real Romany. Huddled in the grass by the woman's side was a pair of small terriers. Two young girls and a small child were also sitting by the fire.

Beyond the camp-fire the three bow-top vans were pulled into a clearing beside the track. Their colours and decoration were magnificent and it was obvious by their immaculate appearance that they were well cared for. There was also a flat waggon which I afterwards discovered was for collecting firewood and materials for basket-making. Further along the drove the travellers' fine horses – two greys and two skewbalds – were tethered.

This was indeed a sight to gladden the heart, for having been born in a cottage on the downs and blessed as a baby by an old Gypsy lady (more of this later), I have always had an affinity with Gypsies. My apprehension at intruding on the privacy of the travellers was quite unnecessary. They were pleased to talk and I discovered that they wintered on the downs every year and in early spring moved on, making their way to the Cotswolds for the Horse Fair at Stow-on-the-Wold. Following this they travel south again to Dorset for the Great Steam Rally.

The drove on which the travellers were camped follows the line of the downs from Shaftesbury to Salisbury Race Plain. They said they had lost one of their favourite and most sheltered camp-sites as it had recently been fenced off and made into a bull pen. Originally it was a piece of rough ground with bramble and hawthorn bushes; some of the bigger hawthorns provided good shelter for the vans. At one time the piece of land had been a sheep-rest when the drovers walked their flocks along the narrow ways to the fairs and markets, and contained a dewpond. So much of this annexation is happening, with the farmers pushing out their fences and expropriating land from the droves.

As dusk approached, the bitter wind cut across the open downs bringing the odd flake of snow. When I departed the travellers were erecting a framed tent for extra shelter. Leaving the camp behind in the twilight I felt as if I had been privileged with a brief glimpse of life as it might have been on the drove in days gone by.

These were the first Romanies travelling in this manner with horse-pulled vans that I had seen for twenty years. With the increasing traffic on the roads and vanishing grass verges the droves and patches of common land are all that is left for them to camp on.

During the week that followed there was a covering of snow. Once again I visited the drove only to find the travellers had gone. All that remained to show where they had been was a small pile of charcoal from the camp-fire. Feeling disappointed I soon realised that they could not possibly have travelled far in such conditions and, looking around, I saw the wheel-tracks and hoof-prints in the snow leading into the wooded entrance of the drove on the opposite side of the road. A five-minute walk brought me to their new camp, a more sheltered place with high bushes. A little girl wearing a pretty flowered skirt with frills was outside playing in the snow. This time two excited terriers came barking towards me followed by a young boy who caught and gathered them up in his arms. The bantams were still strutting around and scratching in the snow.

The Romany woman, who today was wearing a thick tweed cardigan, was washing up beside the camp-fire. The man appeared from inside the tent and we discussed the cold. He said they preferred the higher, drier ground even though they were more exposed as lower down they would have to contend with wet and dampness under-foot.

That day they had been to Shaftesbury travelling by way of the drove on their horse and four-wheeled cart. A journey too had been made to the farm in the valley to collect water, which they had to do every day.

It was obvious from the strings of pegs hanging up to dry out that the travellers were not idle during their winter stay on the drove. The Gypsy man also wove baskets, examples of which I saw as he had just finished three. These baskets, which were special orders for people in the village, were in different shapes – round, oblong, and square. They were woven with flat ropes of straw and the brambles which I had seen on my first visit were incorporated into their making. It was agreed that he would make a round one for me which I would collect before they moved on.

Beyond their camp there were deeper drifts of snow on the track. The carpet of white emphasized the undulating hills and wide expanses. Everywhere red-wings and fieldfare were devouring the remaining berries on the hawthorns.

The travellers' horses, all warm and snug with their blankets on, were tethered at intervals along the track firmly secured by long chains with little padlocks. These gentle creatures with soft brown eyes and sturdy straight legs came up to nuzzle me as I passed by, an indication I felt of the owner's kindness in handling and looking after his horses.

Gypsy horses wintering on Shaftesbury Drove.

Returning through the camp as the light began to fade, all was quiet – the bantams had gone to roost on the axles beneath the vans. The flap of the tent was open and, inside, the man was lighting a stove. The woman was sitting on the edge of a double bed which was covered by a colourful patchwork quilt. On a small table lay a Holy Bible. As the temperature was already below freezing they would certainly need the stove for warmth. Stopping to pass a few words before leaving, and with a promise to visit again before they moved on, I returned to the car just as the sun sank below the horizon.

Due to heavy snow which drifted and blocked some of the higher roads it was two weeks before I was able to return to the downs to see how the travellers had fared during the snow and very low temperatures. Leaving the low ground to climb the hills I encountered banks of snow left from the blizzard, dirty and petrified against the sides of the road. On approaching the Romany camp I was just in time to see the man and woman leaving. They had one of their big grey horses harnessed to a colourfully painted flat trap. No sooner had they jumped aboard than the horse set off at a fast trot along the drove and, lifting its legs in a very hand-some manner, was lost from sight in a few minutes.

The two older girls were standing by the tent; one was very shy and soon disappeared inside after a short chat, but her sister was more talkative. She was a pretty girl wearing a blue and white spotted dress and a suede jacket to keep out the cold wind. A blue headscarf held back her long hair showing to advantage her Egyptian-style ear-rings.

We were joined by the boy I had seen on my previous visit. After a while he disappeared into one of the vans and brought out my completed basket. It was beautifully made with a sturdy handle, and the inside was woven in such a way as to form a swirling pattern. It was a fine example of the skills of these people.

On asking about the welfare of the horses during the snow the boy replied that they had found shelter behind the bushes and with their thick coats were able to cope very well. He said that as soon as the spring weather comes they will be moving on to find fresh keep for the horses, and head towards Stow for the Horse Fair.

During the weeks that followed I made several visits to the Romany camp and each time received a warm welcome. The Gypsies were very proud of the fact that for twenty-five years they were the only family travelling with horses in the South of England. All the children were born in a van on the road.

Over the past few years more and more Romanys have reverted back to the old way of life following where possible the old droves and carters' tracks. These byways across the downs are often short cuts but, more importantly, they enable horse and Romany to travel at the same pace away from traffic and fumes. They can enjoy the countryside and at the end of the day camp in some secluded corner under the shelter of a hedge. It is in the seclusion of these bushes a Romany van will stand its presence detected only by a curl of smoke carried on the wind.

Whilst once again motoring along a downland road I rounded a bend and saw several big horses tethered along a grass verge. These lovely animals with their sturdy legs, shaggy with feathery hair, were secured with long chains. A few hundred yards further on there were four bow-top vans parked in a clearing off the road. Nestling in a glade they were most colourful against the green leafy backcloth. The windows of each van had white lace curtains, crisp and clean. On investigation they proved to belong to a Romany family who were back on the road again after seven years of having been housed. The Gypsy man came to meet me with his little rough-coated terrier called *Jukel* (Romany for dog). As we walked back to the camp he showed me a small copse which was reputed to be haunted. He said it was there that, a long time ago, a Gypsy was murdered.

When we reached the camp-fire I met his wife, two

of their daughters and small grandson. The woman, who was cheerful and friendly, was wearing a long skirt and bright, patterned blouse. The Gypsy man himself looked flamboyant with his dark trousers, red shirt and neckscarf.

Whilst we were talking, their two younger daughters came down from the wood carrying a big ivy-covered branch. One of the girls said she had her own horse of which she was very fond but had experienced two bad scares with it. One was when the horse, tethered along the roadside, became very ill after eating wild parsnip. It was discovered that the horse was allergic to the herb. She said the horse was ill for a long time but with constant attention he eventually recovered. The other scare was the time when the horse snatched and ate some green yew whilst on the road. She said that she sat up all that night with the animal but he suffered no ill-effects. It would probably have been a different story if the yew had been in a state of decay for then it is highly poisonous to animals and only a small amount would prove fatal.

After sitting around the camp fire talking for nearly an hour I was taken to a small clearing about a quarter of a mile along the drove. There I was shown a mare with her new foal. After the Gypsy man had checked that they had sufficient grass and water we returned along the track. By the depth of the hedge and the variety of trees and shrubs it was obvious that the drove was very old. As we walked along, the man named every bush and berry that he saw.

Not very long after that visit it was my pleasure to see the family once again – this time on the road coming down through the village of Downton. A very impressive sight it was with the Gypsy man walking beside the leading horse and his daughters following each at the head of her own horse and van with a young girl riding bareback one of the heavy trace horses at the rear. They were heading for the route over Wick Down and through the dark and sinister wood of Great Yews leading to the main Blandford Road and the Dorset Steam Fair.

It was March before I returned to see if the family on the downs was still there. The weather had been bad during January and February but now it had turned mild and spring-like and I knew they would soon be on the road again heading for Stow. It was a pleasant walk in the warm spring sunshine and the drove being situated along the top of the hills I could look down across the fields to the village below. Larks were soaring overhead, cheering me with their sweet songs.

On reaching the camp I saw the Romany man busy working on his two-wheeled trap. He was colourfully dressed in a claret pullover and waistcoat with his favourite pink silk scarf *diclo* around his neck. Beneath his trilby hat his longish hair was light auburn, as were his moustache and sideburns.

The woman and little girl were sitting beside the fire behind a shelter of sticks and dried grass for although the sun was bright the wind was still chill. I joined them on the ground around the fire which was rather a smoky one of damp gorse wood. I had one of the dogs curled up on my lap and the other beside me. We talked of fires and woodsmoke and the man related how at one time when camping near the New Forest they would collect bundles of charred *fuz* (gorse) sticks after a Forest fire. These sticks they called 'blacklegs'.

The subject then changed to the drove in spring when the flowers were out and glow-worms shone from the banks at night; where in summer to look for the bee orchids, and the juiciest wild raspberries. He said that Wiltshire was once famous for its wild raspberries especially near the grandstand on the Race Plain.

I stayed until the smoke made my eyes water and, as I left the camp, there were calls of 'goodbye' from inside the tent where the sisters were talking together. One of the young girls put her head around the tent flap and her silver ear-rings caught the sunlight making them glint and sparkle. Lying on the track outside the camp was a horse-shoe; I picked it up and said to the man 'a lucky horseshoe' to which he replied, 'You can have that, it has been all the way to Stow and back' – a double lucky horseshoe with a Romany blessing.

Several winters have now passed since my first meeting with the Romany family. During this time, together with my husband Arthur, I have spent many happy hours with them around the camp-fire. A memorable occasion was a cold December afternoon just a week before Christmas. Days of zero temperatures had made the ground hard and, in sheltered places, the frost lay like snow. Overhead the sky was clear but in the valley the fog hung around the trees waiting to rise again as evening approached.

In a small copse high up on the downs we found the travellers gathered around their campfire busily making holly wreaths. Twigs and branches were placed against a clump of bushes to provide shelter from the wind. Scattered about the ground were sprigs of holly, pieces of evergreen, and bits of moss. Propped against a tree was a frame made from twigs and hanging on it were several completed wreaths. The woman planned to sell these in the neighbouring town. The topic of conversation amongst the womenfolk was the various ways to decorate the wreaths. Some used sprigs of holly berries whereas another favoured Christmas roses.

The men, who were not included in this activity, were sitting and standing apart. The Romany man was playing a mandolin whilst the boy strummed his guitar. Their voices singing songs of the travellers resounded through the little copse and the rhythm of Gypsy music carried far on the cold December air. One of the girls, who was standing silhouetted against the pale sky at the edge of the wood, her light brown hair falling over her shoulders and her nimble fingers weaving holly in to a wire frame, came to sit by the fire and, with a sweet voice, joined in the singing.

Sitting by the warmth of the camp-fire, viewing the

scene over the flickering flames, the feeling of approaching Christmas was very strong.

All too soon the light began to fade as the half-moon rose over the hill and shone into the copse. The travellers were suddenly on their feet and there was a buzz of activity around the camp. There were bantams to feed and horses to attend to and the stoves inside the bow-tops to be lit for the night. All this had to be done before darkness fell as the travellers' only means of lighting was candles. We made our farewells with a promise to visit them again in the New Year.

How healing to the mind it is after trying to cope with the stress and tensions of everyday living to spend an hour or so with these happy contented people who want nothing more from life than to follow their seasonal routine of travelling between the Horse Fairs and Steam Rallies.

On the Road

THE HIGHLIGHTS OF THE TRAVELLERS' year are the Horse Fairs. In the spring and autumn the Gypsies from the south head towards the Cotswolds where they converge at Stow-on-the-Wold for the twice-yearly event. On fair day the whole town is a buzz of excitement with everyone dressed in their best and often traditional clothes. The women's cross-over front aprons (*joddakais*), in black silk-like material with elaborately embroidered pockets, are most attractive. At one time they were worn with the very handsome Luton boots; these high black boots were laced all the way down the front. The travellers meet and exchange news whilst in the public house, or *kitchema*, many a yarn is told.

The main car park in the small town of Stow is filled with the showy caravans of the mechanized travellers. At the top of the town a special road is set aside for the Gypsies and their horses. The families camp side by side on the wide grass verge each with their camp-fire lit and kettles and pots steaming. It is here that the horse trading takes place with the animals for sale being run up and down the road to show them off to their best advantage.

The horse trade is not as brisk today as it was but with more Romany families taking to the road again the need for good horses is on the increase.

At one time the Romany was skilled at 'faking' a cure

if he had a poor horse which he wanted to look good on the day of the sale. The faking was usually started several days in advance. One old trick was to put pebbles in a bucket and shake them close to the horses head. This was repeated several times until it nearly drove the poor animal mad. Then on the day of the sale it was necessary only to show the bucket to the horse for him to give a good impression of a prancing young animal. This 'fake' cure would probably have only fooled a *gorgio* (non-Romany). Today it is a fact that a traveller prefers to do business with a fellow traveller for he can then be sure of getting a good horse.

In the evening when the trading is finished it is time for the festivities to begin. Groups of friends and relations gather around the campfires and after the evening meal there will be singing and dancing.

Travellers never dance together, but they love to tap dance. To do this a board is laid down on the ground. There is a Gypsy lady over eighty years of age who still does the 'monkey's hornpipe'. This is a leg kicking dance performed down low to the ground very similar to the Cossack style.

On leaving the Cotswolds for their next destination the travellers daily mileage is determined by their horses, from an average of perhaps fifteen miles, or five, if they have a young foal with them. Then a campsite has to be chosen where there is sufficient fodder for the horses, and water available. Whatever the situation the welfare of his horse is always the first consideration of

Opposite above: Group of travellers meeting at Stow on the Wold Horse Fair.
Opposite below: Trotting a horse at the Fair.

the traveller. It is seldom you will see him riding on the van for he will nearly always be walking at the horse's head, leading it by the bridle. When climbing hills frequent stops are made to rest the horses.

I recall following a convoy of caravans climbing a hill on a country road in Hampshire. On reaching the top they pulled into the wide entrance of a market garden to give the horses a few minutes' rest. They were not in any way obstructing the access but were immediately pounced on by the angry owner who, shaking his fist, ordered them off his land, saying they were giving his market garden a bad image. Stopping to see what was happening I was able to argue with the man on the travellers behalf and try to explain that they had only pulled in to rest the horses. Whilst this was happening the horses recuperated and were ready to continue on their way. The market owner was obviously someone who cared little for the welfare of anyone but himself.

The constant travelling covering several miles a day means the Romany horses need frequent shoeing, and as they are often a long distance from a farrier the traveller has to do it himself. On discussing this with the Romany from the drove he said his method was cold shoeing. This means getting the horses hoof dead flat by cutting and the use of a rasp before putting on the shoe. With the hot method the shoe burns the hoof flat as it goes on.

An example of the distance undertaken by the travellers is illustrated by the family from the drove. Every spring after the fair at Stow they take to the

Opposite above: A gypsy horse being shown off at Stow on the Wold Horse Fair.
Opposite below: Horse trading at the Fair.

road and travel down to Dorset to the chalk downland above Weymouth – a distance of some hundred and fifty miles.

From their summer camp they have unbroken views across the downs to the sea beyond. With their painted vans and horses grazing nearby the Romany camp presents a colourful scene against the white chalk hills. At that time of the year the surrounding lanes are laced with wild flowers. Drifts of blue tufted vetch cling to the hedges beneath green wild oats nodding in the salt breezes. Heather carpets the scrubland and it is from here the travellers pick the lucky purple flowers. They carefully tie them into small sprays and the womenfolk hawk them on the busy sea-front at Weymouth.

At the end of summer they set forth once more on the long journey to the Cotswolds for the Autumn Fair before returning to the Wiltshire downs for winter.

When travelling to and fro between the Cotswolds and Dorset the family from the drove follow roughly the same route each time. Sometimes they deviate slightly according to whether they are travelling alone or have joined up with other travellers. Some of the stopping places in hidden lanes are the same ones used by them for generations.

Whilst they are resting along the way the women-folk go hawking in the nearest town or village and the men make pegs and baskets to sell.

As many of the travellers' stopping places are often hidden from the road, or are off the beaten track, they have their own signs to tell others where they are. The signs which are called *patrin* were used much more in former days when there were many more Romany families travelling the roads. The signs were two or three handfuls of grass lying at a short distance from each other or perhaps a few sticks showing the road taken. Another sign frequently used was a cross drawn in the dust or mud by a Gypsy finger, with the long stem pointing out the Romany trail. Another kind of *patrin* used at night was a cleft stick stuck into the hedge at the side of the road, with a bit of stick in the cleft pointing to the way taken. Any stragglers arriving after dark at the cross-roads will quickly find the *patrin* on the left-hand side and know which way to turn. When Gypsies could roam freely in the New Forest they used bits of heather and gorse as their signs. But the true *patrin* is scattered leaves for *patrin* in Romany means leaf of a tree.

This is a Romany tradition which has not been lost over the years and is used today in exactly the same manner as in olden times with individual families adopting their own methods. For instance the *patrin* of the family from the drove is tufts of grass which they flatten to the road by running over them with the wheels of the wagon to prevent the wind blowing them away.

These *patrin* or signs which were used and followed by the first Gypsies on their wanderings across Europe enabled them never to lose each other.

In former days, when the Gypsy pulled in to camp for the night, he would sometimes put his horses into a field, without the farmer's permission, to graze for the night. This was known as *poov a gris*. First the traveller had to make sure that there were no other animals in the field. This he could usually tell by walking around the edge of the field looking for fresh dung, and by standing quite still and listening. He also had to check for holes in the hedges, and then in the morning be sure to take the horses out of the field before daylight.

These days the farmers will quite often allow the travellers to graze their horses for short periods in exchange for small services on the farm. One traveller that I know is an expert hedge-layer, and often will time his journeys with the knowledge of work ahead.

Open bow-top caravan in a camp in Cranborne Chase.

In spring and summer the Romany life appears idyllic, wandering along the lanes camping beside bluebell woods and eating outside in the sunshine. But in the winter-time it is a different matter altogether for there are so many things to contend with and to take into consideration. For example, when the temperatures are very low it is a problem to keep the water from freezing, and when it is wet, sometimes with endless days of rain, their washing cannot be dried. Not only the washing but firewood also – with so much depending on the fire for warmth, cooking, drying and airing, it is essential to keep the wood dry. One of the places for storing it is beneath the van. Not even a hot drink can be had in the morning until the fire is lit on which to boil the kettle.

If there is a prolonged wet spell the traveller may prefer to camp on high ground but this means he will be exposed to strong winds and sometimes gales with very little shelter. But he would rather that than the mud and water underfoot on the low ground.

An example of the hard life of the traveller was revealed one afternoon recently when I visited a family camped high up on the downs. After days of rain the morning had been bright and sunny but with dark clouds threatening on the horizon. I took a short cut across a field to the camp and was greeted by the sight of a wood fire burning with the kettle over it. There was quite a strong wind blowing and only a few leafless bushes sheltered the family sitting around the fire. There were clouds gathering overhead and big spots of rain began to fall. Everyone scrambled to put cooking utensils beneath the van. The Romany lady scooped up the burning wood from the fire on a shovel and transferred it to the stove in the wagon. She went back to the outside fire which was now just glowing embers and from a basket took some dry twigs which she broke up and placed on the hot ashes, she then knelt on the ground and blew as hard as he could. This rekindled the fire despite the rain and the kettle was put back on and we were soon drinking mugs of hot sweet tea inside the cosy van.

Not long after this our peace was shattered by a strong gust of wind which caught the van side and rocked it precariously. This was followed by a flash of lightning and a clap of thunder, heavy rain and hail.

It was severe whilst it lasted with several more flashes and bangs, but it soon moved away and the rain eased.

The washing spread upon the bushes, which had been almost dry before the rain started, was now soaking wet again. But the Romany family said the weather did not worry them in the slightest. It is only those born into the travelling life who can cope with all the adversities it brings.

Gypsies of days gone by

MY AFFINITY WITH THE TRAVELLING folk probably began at the age of three weeks when a blessing was muttered over me in words of Romany by an old Gypsy lady.

My mother tells the story of how the lonely family cottage high up on the downs of Salisbury Plain had a field at the back which bordered on to a Romany encampment. Inside the compound the Sheen family had their vans drawn around in a circle with a camp fire in the centre. The smoke could always be seen curling upwards through the trees as the fire was kept burning night and day. A big stew pot bubbled away over the flames in which simmered a mixture probably including turnips, wild onions, nettles, any edible fungi such as mushrooms and particularly blewits, a mixture of wild herbs and, of course, rabbit or sometimes pheasant.

The Gypsy women sat around the fire making pegs and paper roses to hawk from door to door, whilst Granny Sheen sat smoking her clay pipe. My father, who was himself a pipe smoker, was always interested to know what Granny Sheen was smoking. He remembers that some times it would be dried oak leaves and another time dried coltsfoot leaves.

The men-folk would ride in brightly painted traps pulled by their sturdy, coloured horses to the village collecting rags and scrap iron.

One day Granny Sheen, who did not often leave the

camp-fire, knocked on the door of the cottage and said she would like to see the baby. She lifted me from my cot into her arms and muttered words in Romany. Seeing the look of apprehension on my mother's face she said, "Don't worry – I blessed not cursed her, it is an old Romany custom when there is a new baby in the house."

During my parents' stay on the downs the Sheen family proved to be good friends. There were occasions when my father's business kept him away for several days which meant that my mother was alone. At these times the Gypsy family kept a watch on the cottage and if they did not see smoke rising from the chimney one of the young lads, either Eli or Henry, would call to see if my mother was alright.

The field behind the cottage belonged to grandfather, and across it was a well-worn path made by the Gypsies on their moonlight poaching trips. Although grandfather knew of this he turned a blind eye and was often offered one of his own rabbits for sixpence. Being partial to rabbit-pie he usually accepted and brought the rabbit back to the cottage for my mother to cook. She always called it poachers pie. Sometimes the Gypsies gave her rabbits in exchange for water which they drew daily from the pump to take back to their camp.

This compromise by grandfather to allow the Gypsies to poach over his land resulted in good relations between Romany and *Gorgio* with both families living peacefully side by side, each pursuing its own way of life.

Although the Sheens lived permanently in their compound on the downs there were other families in South Wiltshire which were constantly on the move. When they were travelling the Gypsies followed the old droves and carters' tracks across the down. Whilst they were resting for a few days along the droves they were not idle. The men-folk would sit around the fire whittling pieces of wood for making clothes pegs. They also made flowers from coloured crepe paper which they attached to sprays of green prickly Butchers Broom.

When they were on the move again and came to a town or village the women would hawk the pegs and flowers from door to door. These were carried in a big basket together with other items according to season. Perhaps there would be rabbits or, in spring-time, bunches of flowers picked from the woods or downs – snowdrops, primroses, cowslips, dainty wild daffodils. Lace and ribbons bought by them for a few pence would also be in the basket, and around Christmas time bunches of holly and holly wreaths. If a Gypsy woman was successful in selling something to the lady of the house she would then ask her if she had any old clothes or rags she could have. Or perhaps she might say that the lady had an interesting hand and would she like her fortune told. Sometimes, if it was a winter's day, the Gypsy would say how cold she was and could she trouble the lady for a hot drink.

As a rule the Gypsy women, although persistent to the point of annoyance, were likable enough, but sometimes there would be a disagreeable one. When I was a child a neighbour had the misfortune to encounter one such Gypsy. A misunderstanding between them as to whether the Gypsy should return for rags ended with a curse being placed on the unfortunate occupant. From that day on our neighbour's health deteriorated – she became tired and thin and eventually died in her sleep. The doctor could find no apparent reason for her illness. Some people said it was the Gypsy's curse; perhaps it was or was not – that remains a mystery.

Another curse by angry Gypsies was placed on the door of the little church of Odstock. The tiny village of Odstock, with its cottages of flint and stone, is situated over the hills three miles south of Salisbury.

At one time a Gypsy called Joshua Scamp lived with his family in a chalk hollow in the village. It so happened that Joshua was wrongly accused of horse stealing, and in 1801 was hanged in Salisbury market place and later buried in the churchyard at Odstock. His Gypsy people were outraged at this and each year on the anniversary of his death they met at the Yew Tree Inn where they drank to his memory before walking to the churchyard to gather around his grave. Each year the Gypsies spent more and more time at the Inn and afterwards caused a disturbance at the church.

Eventually there was a conspiracy between the parson and his church-wardens to lock the church door. They also pulled up a briar rose which had been planted on the Gypsy's grave. When the day arrived and the Gypsies marched from the Inn to the church, only to find the door locked against them, they were furious. An old Gypsy woman jumped on to the wall and shrieked out a string of curses, one of them being that anyone who locked the church door again would die within the year. A parson did lock the door afterwards, and he died before the year was out. Coincidence? I wonder. Following that, the new vicar unlocked the door and threw the key into the nearby river where it remains to this day.

Salisbury market square was the traditional meeting place of the Gypsies from the surrounding districts. The big marble horse drinking-trough was where they gathered on market days to have a yarn and meet with friends and relations.

There was an old Gypsy man with long dark curls down to his shoulders and a red scarf around his neck. With his flamboyant appearance he and the Gypsy women carrying their baskets of wild flowers mingled with the general bustle to contribute to the colourful scene.

Some years ago I once again came into contact with the Gypsies that lived on the rolling chalk downs of Wiltshire. They were the Cooper family whose camp was in a leafy lane high above the city of Salisbury. Old Mr. Cooper, head of the family, was well known to my mother as he called on her at intervals to collect scrap. Wanting very much to paint a picture of a Gypsy van I set out one day to visit the Coopers.

It was a June afternoon – cool and overcast – as I rode over the downs. My mount, a skewbald pony called England, had been jumpy since starting out. He first shied at the spinning wheel of a bicycle which had fallen over and then decided to take off across a golf course so it was no surprise when, turning into the old Ox Drove, he stopped suddenly and refused to move.

I tied the pony to a gate-post and approached the Gypsy camp on foot. I could not get very close as there were five fierce looking dogs tied up at intervals along the lane, all barking and straining at their leashes; a shout from old Henry who was unharnessing his horse, having not long returned from market, soon quietend them and I was able to go right into the camp.

Henry & Lilian Cooper and their bender tent near Salisbury.

What a delightful sight greeting me for it was no ordinary Gypsy settlement but a traditional Romany camp out of the past complete with a painted van and a primitive bender tent which I thought had ceased to exist. The construction of this tent particularly interested me as it was identical to a description given in a then recent newspaper article telling of one that was pitched on waste ground in Southampton fifteen years before.

As I approached, Lilian Cooper appeared from inside the tent. She lifted the flap of canvas and tucked it back, thereby exposing the framework of hazel wands on which it was built. In the centre was a stove with a stack-pipe going out through the top of the tent. The roof was covered with sacks and pieces of carpet.

Inside the tent were Lilian's grand-children fast asleep – two very suntanned Gypsy babies, one petite with black hair, the other chubby and fair.

Lilian herself was colourful in her flowered skirt with its many panels and her long, silver, plaited hair. On admiring her skirt she told me that she had made it herself as she did all her clothes. We talked of many country things. I told her about the badgers which visited my forest garden. She said that although they lived in the open and did a lot of their travelling by night they had never seen a badger. Foxes had often come into their camp, and one they trained as a pet. Before leaving the camp I was able to take several photographs with helped me later with my paintings.

Since those distant days many acres of the Plain have come under the plough, destroying the wild flowers, depriving the hares of their grassy habitat and also making it increasingly difficult for the few remaining travellers to find sites on which to rest their vans. However, there still remains for them the old droves and carters' tracks with their solitude where wild raspberries and harebells grow, and larks sing overhead.

New Forest Gypsies

AT ONE TIME THE GYPSIES were free to roam the New Forest and camp where they liked. It is thought that these wild, dark, mysterious people first came to the forest as far back as the fourteenth century. The leafy glades, wild moorland and green shades with natural springs and trickling streams must have been a paradise for them. However, in recent years officialdom has organized them into compounds and in consequence they have lost their freedom to camp in the Forest.

These compounds were special areas of the forest set aside for the Gypsies. Some were in wooded places whilst others were on open heathland. There were no facilities or sanitation and they had to improvise their own living places, usually tents of shacks.

One well known compound was Shave Green, situated in woodland near Minstead. A typical dwelling there was constructed of old tarpaulins thrown over a wooden framework. The inside was hung with pieces of curtain and in the centre stood an iron stove with a pipe going out through the top of the tent. Another example was a rough shack with perhaps a bed and chair. The fire here would have been a smouldering one on the earthen floor. For this the fuel was usually heather roots or turf.

Conditions in the compounds became bad because the ground was never rested. The grass soon wore away and when it rained it became a quagmire. In contrast to this, the Romany leading his traditional, nomadic way of life could choose his site carefully, taking into consideration whether it was sheltered and if the ground was well drained. Staying just for a few days no damage was done and the only evidence of a camp was the remains of the camp-fire.

The siting of some compounds was totally unsuitable. The one at Millersford Bottom near Fordingbridge was a good example. As the word 'Bottom' indicates, it was in a valley between two heather-clad hills. With the water running off the clay the camp was surrounded by bog. It was here that the Sheen family lived, still using the old Gypsy bell-type tents.

Painting of New Forest Gypsies by Eryl Vize.

Eventually all the compounds were condemned and the Gypsy families moved elsewhere; some were even housed. Fordingbridge is still a stronghold of many Gypsy families, particularly the Coopers. They have perhaps been more fortunate than others for they have been able to distribute themselves in caravans, albeit modern ones tucked away on common land, or in wooden huts overlooking the Forest and some even in cottages. More unfortunate families in other parts of the Forest have ended up in council houses on the edge of built-up areas.

My three-hundred-year-old thatched cottage at Abbots Well near Fordingbridge is an original forester's cabin and one of the few left standing. It nestles beneath the hill under the laurels in a corner of the garden where it is now used as an artist's studio. The modern cottage in which we live was built in the wild garden that once surrounded the old cabin.

In the past the cottage has been lived in by foresters, artists, writers and more recently by herbalist and friend of the Romanies, Juliette de Bairacli Levy. She stayed in the cottage with her two children for three years whilst working on her herbal remedies. Juliette was born of Turkish blood and lived an open air life similar to that of the Romany. During her sojourn in the cottage she and her two children bathed daily in a forest pond across the heather from the cabin. Even in winter and often at night by the light of an oil lantern and sometimes barefoot they visited the pond. Foresters tell of hearing their laughter carried on the night air.

Herself a colourful character, Juliette had befriended the Romanies in numerous foreign lands. Back in her Abbots Well cottage she was visited by many of the forest Gypsies, some of who were at that time living in nearby compounds. One old lady in particular came regularly to help Juliette with her herbal research. Her name was Eiza Cooper and she revealed to her many of the Romany secrets concerning herbs and their uses.

Several years later when the cottage came into our possession Eiza still called occasionally on the pretence of collecting rags and old clothes. I think she liked to see again the cottage where she spent so much of her time with Juliette. Eiza, who admitted to being over eighty, still worked at the market garden where she lived in a caravan. Together with other local Gypsies, she hoed the weeds from between the rows of lettuce and strawberry plants.

The custom among all Gypsy women hawking from door to door was to ask for a drink. Eiza was no exception and she always came in for a cup of tea. Her suntanned face, furrowed and lined with years of living and working outdoors, was framed by two grey plaits looped and fastened behind her ears. Whilst she sipped her tea, which she always tipped into the saucer first, she would relate how she told Juliette all about herbs.

Often Eiza brought a small gift in exchange for the old clothes, usually wild flowers – primroses from the hedgerows or wild daffodils from the woods. She also told me stories of the old days when they could camp in the Forest. She said she loved to sit by the camp-fire smoking 'baccy' and, with a ball of string and a hook, weave nets for the menfolk to use when rabbiting. Sometimes she said the nets would be over a hundred yards long. They were placed over the rabbit burrows; then on a windy night when the rabbits could not hear, the Gypsies set their lurchers on them. The rabbits, being unable to escape down their holes, fell easy prey to the dogs.

On Eiza's very last visit we exchanged gifts. For a miniature painting of forget-me-nots she gave me a small cameo pendant which I still treasure to this day.

A few years after Eiza's death a handsome Gypsy boy

came to the gate seeking garden work. Looking very sun-tanned against his dark blue shirt and red neck-scarf he proved to be old Eiza's grandson Wally Cooper. His hair was dark and curly and when he spoke he looked directly at you with cool grey eyes. He was fascinated to see the inside of the cottage where his 'gran' had spent so much of her time with Juliette. He said he was proud of his 'gran' and also of his Gypsy origins.

Another dear lady who sometimes visited my Abbots Well cottage was Annie Cooper, who lived in the neighbouring village of Hyde. She was fortunate enough to be able almost to follow her old way of life by living in a caravan, albeit a modern one as opposed to a Romany van, tucked away in a secluded corner on a piece of common land adjoining the forest. All her water she had to get daily from a well on the common, and for her stove she collected dead gorse wood.

Although in her eighties she was a very active lady with many interests. She would walk into Fordingbridge and back each morning – an over-all distance of three miles. Annie was always colourfully dressed in a long floral skirt and a short coat with bright apron and headscarf. In spring and summer her big basket would be filled with flowers, and at Christmas you could see her walking along the lanes to Fordingbridge pushing a pram brimming over with holly. The old Gypsy lady followed the tradition of making holly wreaths, the moss for the foundations of which she would gather from the hillside around Abbots Well. She also made pretty crepe paper flowers which the Gypsies traditionally make at Christmas. She had wire for the stems of her flowers but sometimes the prickly butchers broom was used. This is a stiff evergreen which grows in the Forest and

A Romany lady making paper roses at Christmas time.

is so called because at one time butchers used it to scrub their wooden table tops. It is also sometimes referred to as knee-holly. Annie once gave me a posy of her paper flowers which I kept until they became faded and dusty.

Annie had two passions – one was her ponies and the other was collecting paintings. She had a number of ponies on the forest which would come home every day in the winter to be fed. Sometimes she would be outside at five in the morning searching amongst the gorse bushes for a pony which had failed to return the night before. Her favourite was a grey mare called 'Feather' which was well over thirty years old. One day we saw her leading Feather off the forest. She came down over Chilly Hill and up the road to Abbots Well. Knowing how much Annie liked paintings and how fond she was of that particular mare my husband Arthur met her in the lane and suggested that he take their photograph to use as the basis for an oil painting. The old gypsy lady was delighted and posed readily for the photo.

After that she called regularly at the cottage to see how the painting was progressing. During the course of her visits she chose a picture of mine, moorhens by a stream, and a still life painted by my father. She said one of her treasured possessions was a drawing by Augustus John, but as it was of a nude she could not have it hanging in her caravan because it would not be fit for her grandchild to see when she visited her. The drawing was given to Annie by one of John's sons after the artist's death. Eventually the painting of Annie and Feather was finished and she came to the cottage to collect it. She said that the walk here from her caravan in the cold wind had made her feel dizzy so she went into the cottage and she sat down to rest whilst I made tea. I left her in the good company of a friend who was on holiday from Canada, and later over cups of tea we talked of many things of days gone by.

The old Gypsy lady remembered as a child sitting around a campfire in the forest eating deer stew, and she said she still had her bender tent, cooking pot and kettle from the days when camping on the forest; her dream was to erect the tent again and light a campfire. Annie was delighted with the painting and June took a photograph of her holding it. Later I drove her home; on reaching her van she disappeared behind it and came back with an old iron fender which she wanted me to have in return for the painting. I explained that I had nowhere to put it having the wrong kind of fireplace for a fender, so she decided to keep it and sell it later for five pounds.

At one time the Cooper family were camped along the hedge down the side of Chilly Hill, opposite Abbots Well, a delightful place where curlews call and night-jars whirr at sunset. They had their vans and tents together with carts and animals on the hillside across the valley from our cottage.

Annie's granddaughter was a pretty half-Gypsy girl who had a New Forest pony which she rode everywhere. It was a fine sight to see her galloping bareback through the bracken, her hair streaming in the breeze, jumping over gorse bushes that got in her way.

The love of horses and ponies still survives in the Romany families of today and Forest Gypsies now settled in the area who live in cottages and drive pick-ups, deal in ponies and attend all the New Forest sales.

Until recently, in the small New Forest town of Ringwood, there was a covered livestock market where you could bid for anything from a rabbit to a horse. It was here that Gypsies gathered to buy and sell their horses. Not the big horses at one time associated with the Romanies for pulling their vans but New Forest ponies. Some years ago there was a dealer in the Abbots Well area called Gypsy Peters. A forester neighbour remembers how, during hard weather, he would meet him daily coming up the lane with sacks full of gorse. This furze he would later pound with a mallet to make a forage for the ponies.

Today the Gypsies still deal in ponies which they run on the Forest. For this privilege they have to pay a grazing fee on each animal but the sale of foals in the Beaulieu Roads pony sales more than covers this outlay. Around Fordingbridge the Gypsies have always worked on the land either in the market gardens or the strawberry fields. In the summer it is a common sight to see half a dozen women with colourful aprons and headscarves hoeing between the lettuces and strawberry plants in a market garden at Gorley. Juliette remembers, when living in the cottage, hearing the Gypsies singing whilst working in the fields beyond the garden.

Top: Romany boy on his horse at Stow on the Wold Horse Fair.
Below: Gypsy horse grazing at roadside.

Two sturdy Gypsy horses returning from being watered.

In former days when the Gypsies lived in the forest they picked wild blackberries for the jam factories in the area. Lenn Witt, a forester neighbour, said he used to carry the filled baskets on his horse and cart to a reception depot at Romsey. Here he was given payment – sometimes as much as seventy pounds – to take back to the Gypsy workers.

Apart from the traditional items such as clothes pegs and paper flowers the forest Gypsies also made ash casks for the foresters' mead. The New Forest was once famed for the Old English mead that was brewed by the foresters. This was a very potent brew which often led to drunkenness. There is a lovely story told in the Forest that if a visitor had been unpleasant during his stay he would be given a large drink of mead before his departure in the hope he would fall from his pony before reaching home.

Juliette says in her book *Wanderers In the New Forest* that during her stay in the Abbots Well cottage, the best artificial flowers she had seen anywhere were those made by the New Forest Romanies. The colours she said they had taken from the sunset over the moors. The paper they painted with stripes and used dyed beeswax or wax residue from coloured candles in which to dip the paper flowers.

There are two holly copses across the heath from Abbots Well known as first and second bushes, and long ago these were Romany encampments. There still remains evidence of this in the scrap iron lying around, some half buried, other bits in the middle of bramble bushes – pieces of old prams, bicycles. bedstead, buckets and other items.

Lenn Witt remembers back to the days when the Gypsy women with their long dark hair carried wild produce from the forest in their big calling baskets and hawked from door to door. There would be heather, rabbits, bunches of wild watercress and of course clothes pegs. The watercress was mostly gathered from the wild natural beds in Merrie Thought wood. These beds were in the heart of the wood and were watered by springs and streamlets running off the Forest. The area of the cress-beds was so vast that the Gypsies could fill their baskets without their takings being noticed. Wild flowers in season would also be found in their baskets, such as the early snowdrops, then primroses and wild daffodils gathered from the woods bordering the forest. Although they picked and sold snowdrops the Gypsies themselves were not fond of these flowers and would never take them inside their vans as they feared that to do so would bring them bad luck.

The rabbits in their baskets would probably have been poached as there has always been a plentiful supply in the forest. Windy nights were usually chosen as these conditions were best for the use of ferrets and dogs. Quite often the Gypsies legally helped the farmers by clearing the rabbits from their land for them by using ferrets.

There is a story told by Len Witt about poaching of another kind. Two Gypsy girls he knew walking in the forest when they came upon a wild duck on a pond. One girl jumped fully clothed into the water and caught the astonished duck before it realized what was happening. That night it was much enjoyed in the cooking pot back at the Gypsy camp. He goes on to tell of how the Gypsy boys often caught wild duck for the pot but they used slings and stones and sometimes bows and arrows. Deer stew may have been in the cooking pot as the Gypsies also poached the deer. They stalked them and hid behind trees jumping out on the unsuspecting animals and killed them.

November the 26th is the traditional date on which the Gypsies are allowed to start picking holly to sell at the markets and to make wreaths. At one time they filled their sacks with moss gathered from the boggy paths on the side of the hill above Abbots Well. This they used as the foundation of the wreaths. But it is no longer permissible to pull moss or any other plant.

As Fordingbridge and Ringwood still have many Romany families living in the area there is naturally from time to time a Gypsy funeral. It is not unusual at this time for the traffic on the route to be halted as it is the custom for the funeral cortège to follow the hearse to the church on foot. It is a moving sight to see the procession of mourners with everyone dressed entirely in black – a mark of respect which is still strictly adhered to by this unique race of people.

Fordingbridge will always remain associated with the New Forest Romanies for it was here that their champion and friend Augustus John lived. The famous painter, known to the Gypsies as Sir Gustus, was looked upon by many of them as their King. As President of the Gypsy Lore Society he fought very hard for these people to retain their rights to travel and settle where they liked in the Forest. However, bureaucracy ensured that these ancient rights would not continue despite other traditional uses, such as hunting, that were allowed to continue.

A Leeds square Bow van.

A Gypsy Way of Life

THE ROMANY PEOPLE HAVE INHERITED the urge to travel and they are not happy unless free to do so. The authorities have tried to house or put them into compounds but, with a few exceptions, this has not been successful. These nomadic people are never happier than when they are at one with nature, travelling the lanes and sitting beside their campfires under the stars.

The homes of the travellers are colourfully painted wagons. There are four types of vans – Leeds, Reading, Burton, and Ledge. The Leeds are distinctive by their hooped-shaped canvas roofs usually green, and variously known as roll-tops, barrel-tops, or bow-tops. There is also a square canvas-top version of the Leeds. The Reading is a tall stately wagon with large wheels, the body being wider at the roof and carrying a wealth of carving. This shape of van is the one usually portrayed in paintings or pictures of Gypsies.

The Ledge wagons derive their name from the shape of the body which overhands to form a ledge in the interior which acts as a long seat. The wheels are generally smaller than on the Reading and are immediately beneath the body. The Burton vans are square and heavy looking with sturdy wheels also beneath the body of the van. Their roofs are flat and the sides panelled with ornate carving.

Some of the best examples of these wagons can be

seen at Peter Ingram's Romany Museum at Selborne in Hampshire. The hard work of restoring these vans to their full glory is carried out to perfection by Peter and his small team. Not only the carving and replacements which have to be done but also the intricate painting afterwards. The colours which appear to be traditional for these travellers' homes are a rich wine and dark green with the carving picked out in gold.

One van in particular at the museum which I find very interesting is an old brush van waiting its turn to be restored. It is still in the same condition as when it was found. Along the outside of the van are rows of specially designed brackets in natural carved wood to display the brush heads to their full advantage. It was a van used by a brush pedlar to travel the countryside selling his wares, and I think I am right in saying it is the last one in existence.

I recently saw some fine examples of restoration work carried out by two talented craftsmen, John Pocket and John Picket. John Pocket's Leeds van, which was on display at a country fair in Wiltshire, was painted a striking yellow. This colour scheme produced a pleasing effect against the green surroundings. Also showing at the same fair was a very ornate example of a Leeds van which had been restored by John Picket and was destined for a Gypsy fortune teller.

Whilst walking down a Cornish lane on a hillside close to the sea I came across a very dilapidated Reading van almost hidden beneath the overhanging trees. Venturing to look through the open door and at the same

Opposite above: A fine Reading on display at Fordingbridge Show.
Opposite below: A Burton (Showmans) van in Cornwall.

time call to see if anyone was there I was answered by a North country voice. When the traveller came outside he was eager to relate the history of the old van. He said that it was the oldest Reading in the country and he was going to spend the winter restoring it. I was invited inside and, although I could see it was in a very bad state of repair, the main structure survived which would be something to work upon. It so happened that the traveller, whose name was Barney, was a skilled coach builder and maintained that he could build a Reading van from scratch in three months, so working on this one would not take as long. The main problem he said was finance – parts such as new wheels, axles and springs cost a lot of money.

It was the first time I had been in a Reading van and I was surprised by the height from the ground. Inside it was very dim with the only light coming from the open door as the windows were covered by the tarpaulin protecting the van. Even in its derelict state it felt cosy and safe. Sitting in front of the warm stove with the smell of woodsmoke I felt the atmosphere of the past and tried to visualise the families whose home it had once been.

Barney himself, though a young man, could have been a traveller from the past. He wore a waistcoat over a crisp white shirt, and on one hand every finger was adorned with rings in gold and silver.

I was once invited to tea in one of the Burton show-mans' vans when it was at its winter quarters in a field near Salisbury. The inside was immaculate and filled

Opposite: Front view of a bow-top fully restored by John Picket for use by a gypsy fortune teller.

with beautiful china and glass. In one corner was a shiny black coal-stove with a stainless steel chimney stack which went out through the roof. There were various cupboards and lockers and a panelled door led to the sleeping quarters at the far end. One corner cupboard displayed a set of beautiful plates, each one hand-painted with a picture of a horse-drawn wagon similar in shape to the one we were in. The owner was a jolly lady who had spent her life travelling with the Fair, said she had the china specially made to remind her of life in her father's time when horses were used to pull the wagons. She gave me a fascinating account of her family who had always been travelling folk.

On another occasion just a few days before Christmas with a bitter wind blowing over the downs, I climbed the steps of another showman's van. This one was situated on the highest point of an ancient drove commanding spectacular views in all directions. Inside the van it was warm and cosy with a long padded seat stretched before the glow of a coal fire in the range opposite. From the tiny side oven came the smell of potatoes baking in their jackets. An open door at the end of the van revealed a small bedroom where I glimpsed a double bed covered by a frilly pink bed-spread with a patchwork quilt over the top.

An outstanding feature of the showman's vans is the heavy engraved glass panels in the doors and dividing sections. The mirrors are also engraved with pictures in the corners and around the edges.

But it is the Leeds bow-top vans which are used by the families travelling the countryside today. The wagons are often bought in bad repair at the fairs and are restored by the travellers as they camp along the way using whichever colour paint they happen to have.

Putting final decorative touches to a repainted van.

*Above: Water carriers on step of restored van: Gypsy
Museum, Selborne.*
*Opposite above: Peter Ingram, restorer of Romany vans at
his Gypsy Museum, Selborne.*
*Opposite below: Sample of a typical cooking range used in
larger gypsy vans.*

The interiors of these vans are smaller than the show-mans' but they are very colourful with the woodwork along the sides of the sleeping area decorated with painted flowers. Often the material used between the ribs and roof canvas blends with and compliments the exterior overall colour of the van.

Usually there is a tiny stove near the entrance with a pipe going up and out through the canvas roof. This pipe, which gets very hot, helps to heat the van and also airs any damp clothes hung near to it. The sleeping quarters is at the far end of the wagon in two tiers giving a top and bottom bed. The sheets are often lace-trimmed, sometimes with a complete lace bedspread over a brightly coloured or patchwork quilt.

The Gypsies love flowers and you will find a bunch of wild flowers according to the season in a small vase or jam jar in the van. There are exceptions though, for travellers are superstitious about taking certain blossoms inside; snowdrops in particular. Nevertheless they do have them outside the van. I can still visualise a green bow-top, which had posies of primroses and bluebells on ledges beside the door, resting under a hawthorn tree clustered in blossom. At Christmas the flowers are replaced by holly.

To team up with these colourful vans are the big Gypsy horses which pull them from place to place. To take the weight of the wagons up hill and down the horses have to be heavy and strong. These lovely animals, with their sturdy legs fringed with feathery hair, are gentle creatures despite their size and are obedient to the Romany's every command. I love to see the Gypsy man from the drove riding his big piebald, and leading another coloured but smaller mare across the chalk downs above Weymouth. The small mare is also taken at midday down the grassy lane to the valley below to meet the Romany lady from the bus, tired after selling her heather on the sea front, to give her a lift up the hill back to the camp.

The names for the horses are all appropriately chosen – Prince and Buddha because of size and nobleness; Sherpa for his ease in climbing the hills, and Bluebell, as she was born beside a bluebell wood.

Interior of a Romany van: Gypsy Museum, Selborne.

The horses are unharnessed and tethered on long chains to graze and rest. The travellers then light a campfire over which they boil a kettle to make their *mutramengri* (tea). A Romany fire is never flaring with high flames but is rather a smouldering one inclined to make smoke. Pushed into the ground beside the fire and leaning towards the centre is the crane, a piece of iron crooked at the end to hold a kettle or cooking pots over the fire.

The *yog* as the fire is called in Romany, is the focal point of the camp. Apart from its use for cooking, the fire is a gathering place with the travellers sitting around it on upturned boxes or any available object that can be used as a seat. There are many superstitions connected with the fire, one being that you should never walk between it and the Romany. It is even used in some Gypsy wedding ceremonies when the bride and groom leap over the flames with their hands joined.

My association with Gypsy camp-fires is strong sweet tea. I have drunk numerous mugs of tea around various camp-fires always from colourfully decorated mugs. The travellers buy these mugs, which are in fine china, at the horse fairs. They vary in pattern according to which design is fashionable at the time. The most recent one I drank from has a wild strawberry pattern on it, and there was also a matching tea pot. There are numerous other designs – a particularly attractive one is a horse and wagon, whilst a horse's head was popular at one time. Whatever the design on the mug it is always worth waiting for. The tea is usually sweet for invariably it has condensed milk from a tin added as Romany camps are often remote and fresh milk is not always available. But the anticipation of a mug of tea is made greater by the slightly longer wait for the kettle to boil over the fire than pressing the button on an electric one. On visiting a traveller in a leafy Cornish lane his camp-fire was not even lit as he had just returned from market. I was fascinated to watch the speed and technique he used to light the fire and get it hot enough to boil a kettle.

Romany boy watching the cooking pot.

Sitting around a campfire is not all tea drinking for the Gypsies as there is work to be done. The men busy themselves making clothes pegs and weaving baskets. There is still a demand for these items not only from the public but for the Romany museums which are in various places around the country. I have come across baskets and pegs made by the family on the drove as far away as Wales.

The women make paper flowers and, at Christmas, holly wreaths which they hawk from door to door. Before they can fill their big baskets and set out to sell their wares they have to obtain a hawker's licence.

However, when work is done and the evening meal finished, that is the time for music and singing. On fine evenings the travellers like to sit beneath the stars in the glow of the fire. As they toss their heads to the rhythm of the music, points of light glint on their gold ear-rings. The Gypsies love gold and it is traditional for them to wear ear-rings. Gypsy children have their ears pierced at a very early age. The usual method is to use a thick needle and a bar of soap or a piece of cork behind the ear to press against. This may sound primitive but it is quite hygenic with the needle used being new. At some weddings a pair of gold ear-rings is given to the bride by the groom as part of the ceremony.

It is customary for a Gypsy woman to keep her maiden name after she is married if she wishes to do so. Some of the well known Romany surnames are Sheen, Cooper, King, Boswell, Lee, Draper, Peters, Smith and Wells. Eiza Cooper told how New Forest children had two Christian names – one non-Gypsy for school and one Romany for the family. For example Henry at school could have been Eli at home.

Although Romany is no longer spoken as a language there are many words still used by them. As some travellers still cannot read or write these remaining words of this secret language are passed on to the children by word of mouth.

Here is a small example from the vocabulary:

Atchin–Tan	Stopping Place
Ava	Yes
Aladge	Ashamed
Atch	To Stay, Stop
Atraish	Afraid
Bashadi	A Fiddle
Bavol-angro	A wind fellow, ghost

Beano	Born
Bengree	Waistcoat
Bor	A Hedge
Bikhin	To sell
Bokra	A Sheep
Bokkar-engro	A Shepherd
Chavies	Children
Chi	Child
Choon	Moon
Chore	To steal
Churi	Knife
Churi-mengo	Knifegrinder
Cuesni	Basket
Del-engro	A kicking horse
Diklo	Neck-cloth
Dordi-Dordi	Oh dear, Oh dear!
Dukker	To tell fortunes
Drom	Road
Dromengro	Man of the the road
Gorgio	Non-Gypsy
Gry	Horse
Gry-Choring	Horse Stealing
Gry-Engro	Horse Dealer
Hatch	To burn, light a fire
Hotche withchi	Hedgehog
Joddakai	Apron
Jukel	Dog
Karring	Hawking goods
Kekkauvi	Kettle
Kekkauviskey saster	Kettle iron, the hook by which the kettle is suspended over the fire.
Kitchema	Inn
Kore	To hawk goods about
Koring lil	Hawking license
Lav	Word
Lavengro	Man of words
Moomli	Candle

Mush	Man
Mushi	Woman
Mutramengri	Tea
Nevi Wesh	The New Forest
Pani	Water
Peamengri	Teapot
Petul	A Horse-shoe
Petulengro	Blacksmith
Pirry	Pot, Cauldron
Poov	Earth, Ground
Poov a gry	Put a horse in a field at night.
Rai	Gentleman, lord
Rawnie	Lady
Romanes, Romany	Gypsy language
Romany Rye	Gypsy gentleman
Rook	Tree
Rookomengro	Squirrel
Saster	Iron
Shooshi	Rabbit
Swegler	Pipe
Tan	Place, Tent
Tatting	Collecting old clothes
Tuv	Smoke
Vardo	Wagon
Vongra	Money
Wesh	Forest, wood
Welgaulus	A Fair
Weshen Jukel	Fox
Yarb	Herb
Yog	Fire
Zimmen	Broth

Romany Art

THE ARTS AND SKILLS OF the Romanies were and still are put to many uses. Their talents are numerous and, together with time and patience, they produce a wealth of beautiful things.

With agile fingers they weave and plait the reeds and rushes to make bee skeps and baskets. The Gypsy man from the Shaftesbury drove makes baskets using coils of straw bound with strips of bramble. The bramble stalks are cut from the hedges and tied into bundles to dry. The thorns are then removed and the stalks cut into strips. Using these to bind the straw they also form an attractive pattern to the baskets. The Gypsy man uses the strips of bramble in their natural colour but there are other families who colour the bramble by using dyes.

Many years ago my mother bought two baskets from one of the Turner family hawking at the door. They were trug shape with strips of red and blue bramble woven in. One of the baskets, which was in regular service in the garden holding light tools such as twine and scissors, lasted years before it wore out. The other basket however, having been used to carry flowers only, is still in perfect condition and is now kept to carry herbs needed in the kitchen. At other times the basket stands beside the inglenook in our Forest cottage for others to admire as made by the Gypsies. An interesting postscript to the story of the baskets occurred recently when a friend, who has close connections with the travellers and restores old Romany vans, was visiting us. On seeing the remaining basket he knew exactly where it had originated and related how he had been taught by the family to make the baskets. They were so tightly woven they would hold water.

Sitting one wet afternoon inside the bow-top van of the family on the drove I watched the man preparing the straw for the baskets. Apart from pieces of chaff scattered over the floor the rest of the van was spotless. His mandolin was hung on the roof, and tucked into the ribs of the van was a variety of artificial flowers most of them made from dyed swansdown and feathers. A damp coat was drying beside the hot stove making the air moist which emphasized the smell of the straw. The Romany woman was sitting at the front of the van beside the open canvas flap. Her dark hair, traditionally parted in the centre and plaited, framed her tanned face. Her sharp brown eyes twinkled as frequently she smiled when relating a story. How cosy it was sitting beside the stove looking out at the softly falling rain and listening to the contented clucking of the bantams which were roosting on the shafts just outside the van.

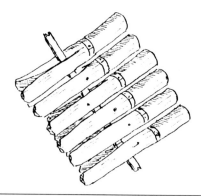

It is fascinating to watch a Gypsy seated on the ground surrounded by wood-shavings making pegs. The rapidity with which he whittles the willow or ash using a very sharp knife is amazing. I was watching the man from the drove making pegs one day when he looked up and said, "Did you know there are seven stages of peg-making?"

First Cut: meaning to cut the wood from the copse.

Second: Chop off – to chop off the brush-wood.

Third: Rind them – to strip off the soft bark or skin.

Fourth: Chop off to peg length.

Fifth: Tin them – put the tin bands around them.

Sixth: Mouth them – slit up to the tin to make the opening.

But that's only six I said.

"Ah," he said with a smile, "the seventh and last stage is the most difficult of all, that's selling them."

When the pegs are finished they are wedged on to a spreader which is a long thin strip of wood, and then hung on the bushes to dry out. They have to be made when the wood is green otherwise they will split. The pegs can be made in the summer or winter. In the summer, to peel the wood is to rind it; in winter it is to shave it.

For the operation of peg-making the craftsman's knife has to be very sharp. The traveller always makes his own knife, the wooden handles of which are usually very ornately carved. One design is a horse's head, and another is in the shape of a Luton boot.

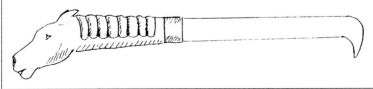

The very sharp knife is put across the peeled wood and driven with a hammer to cut it cleanly into peg lengths.

Usually the wood-shavings are not wasted but are made into chrysanthemum heads. These are then dyed different colours with vegetable dyes and attached to stems made from wire or butchers broom. The latter is also used as stalks for the roses made from coloured crepe paper.

A young traveller I came upon in Cornwall had a versatile talent in Romany art. His name was Nigel Sjholm and he was locally known as the Scandinavian traveller as his father, who had been a seafaring man operating out of Newlyn, had originated from Sweden.

It was interesting to see Nigel's works of Romany art. Apart from making the traditional pegs and wood-shaving flowers he painted old horse-shoes in bright colours with the words 'Good Luck' adorning them. The thing he excelled at was painting the decoration on the bow-top vans. In the few days between meeting him in Marazion and again in Helston he had added a splendid horse to the panel over the door of his van.

Nigel had travelled up to Helston for the annual Harvest market. Helston, which is famous for its Furry Dance, is a quaint little town with fresh water streams running through deep gutters at the sides of the roads. During the market the streets are lined with stalls selling goods of all descriptions. It overflows down below the town into the park where it is joined by a fun fair. There in a corner of the old cattle market the horse sales are held. This was the reason that Nigel had come although he was not intending to sell his own horse. He had in fact not had it very long and, being very young, it was fresh and a handful to control when pulling the van. For this reason Nigel had to keep on the move to provide the horse with enough exercise.

One day, whilst sitting around the camp fire talking to Nigel and admiring his silver-cream lurcher Stigger, he produced a photograph album filled with pictures of other travellers. Amongst them was a photograph of a family well known to us in Hampshire. It was given to him at Stow Fair by a traveller after Nigel had admired his beautiful daughters. It was one of the few occasions that he had visited the Cotswold Horse Fair as normally he travels only around Cornwall.

Nigel Sjholm, a young traveller in Cornwall.

On visiting Nigel two years later at his camp in a hidden Cornish lane I was shown an example of his latest artistic skill. He had been having instruction on weaving wicker baskets and his first effort was a very handsome calling basket. The outer ridge was raised higher in loose looped cane in which the hawker could tuck her bundles of lace and ribbons or sprigs of heather.

It was a memorable afternoon for my husband Arthur and me sitting around his camp-fire drinking mugs of tea together with Barney, another traveller from the same lane.

One skill shared by most Gypsies is that of making holly wreaths at Christmas-time. With a foundation of moss and a base of holly they add additional decoration according to their individual taste. Some use paper roses glazed with the wax of a melted candle to weatherproof them, whilst others included plastic flowers. Olive, the daughter from the family along the drove, adds tiny larch cones with pleasing effect.

With her artistic flair she produces many attractive items such as Victorian posies of dried flowers with lace surrounds, and delightful teasle-faced mice with pearls for eyes and gowns of velvet.

From Olive's skilled fingers I saw examples of exquisite sewing – an apron with intricate gathers of lace adorning it (an apron or *joddakai* is a traditional part of a Romany woman's clothes) and items of patchwork. The largest of the patchwork creations was a quilt which was nearing completion after four-and-a-half years work. Sitting beside the camp fire one cold but sunny February morning I was fascinated to watch the lovely young Romany girl with the colourful quilt spread before her adding the patches one by one. Each little section was cut octagonal shape and stitched over a cardboard form before being added to the main piece.

One of the daintiest pieces of sewing I have seen was a tiny pin cushion hat made with green velvet and

Opposite: A Romany craftsmen at work on a hazel strip basket.

decorated with minute dried flowers. It was the work of Olive's lovely young sister Sarah, who gave it to me as a gift.

Another Gypsy lady who was clever with the needle was Lilian Cooper, a traveller of the chalk downs many years ago. She had hand-sewn all her own clothes and the skirt she was wearing the day I visited the camp was quite lovely. It was long with tiers of frills and panels, and made in a cotton floral print material.

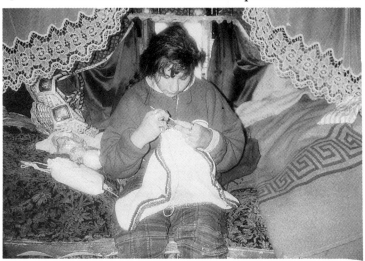

A Romany girl doing her crochet inside a bow-top van, Dorset.

Some Romany art is hidden away and rarely seen. I cannot forget meeting a young Gypsy girl probably in her mid-teens. She was quiet and serious with big dark eyes which shone out of a beautifully sculpted face of high cheekbones. On the rare occasion of a quick smile her perfect white teeth glistened. She wore her dark hair parted in the centre and drawn back close to her face, golden ear-rings highlighting her Romany ori-gins. Her father told her to show me her paintings whereupon she disappeared into one of the vans and later emerged carrying an exercise book. What treasures revealed themselves when she opened back the cover. There on the pages of this little book, drawn with coloured felt tip pens in primitive but unique style, was page upon page of everyday Gypsy life. There were their beloved horses, colourful vans in every detail, and here and there a close-up of some intricate carving on a van. There were scenes from the horse fairs and of the family on the road.

It is not common to see pictures painted by Gypsies. Several years ago great acclaim was given to Eryl Vize for her oil paintings of Romany life. It was mistakenly thought that she was a Gypsy herself as she had written the titles of her work in Romany.

Eryl Vize lived on the picturesque wooded hill across the valley from my cottage. She had the New Forest Gypsies all around her, even camping on her land. Her paintings were bold and colourful, her primitive style captured the wild beauty of the Romanies and their surroundings. She dared to use clear, bright colours where others would have been timid. A Romany *vardo* in golden yellow filled one canvas whilst a raven-haired 'Gypsy Witch, Esmerelda', wearing a scarlet dress adorned another. Eryl Vize's work was admired by Augustus John who bought one of her Gypsy sketches for himself.

Sven Berlin, well known artist and one time friend of Augustus John, also painted Gypsies. For some years he lived as a Romany himself travelling from Cornwall to the New Forest with a horse-drawn wagon.

He spent many hours in the Shave Green compound sketching the Gypsies and capturing their various moods on paper which he later transferred to canvas. The culmination of this was an exhibition of his paintings at the Bladon Gallery in Hampshire. Exhibiting with him was his wife Juanita whose work was mainly of horses. It was a flamboyant occasion with the exhibition being opened by Augustus John and attended by a gathering of Gypsies who came to see the paintings of themselves.

Sample of a hawking basket containing pegs and paper roses.

One talent which is found in most of the travelling folk is that of music and singing. At the end of the day work is forgotten and invariably the evening will finish with either story-telling or a sing-song around the camp-fire. Mandolins, guitars, and violins are amongst the instruments used to provide the music. I once heard the sound of accordion music coming from a lone van standing in a clearing at Grovelly Woods in Wiltshire. The Gypsy woman told of how on moonlight nights her husband would play the accordion and she would sing often until the early hours.

There is no better way to end the day than to relax under the stars before the warmth of the camp-fire and let the imagination drift to the melody of a haunting Gypsy love song. But mostly the songs the Romanies like best are about everyday life and folklore which lend themselves very well to their voices. One song which particularly comes to mind I heard sung by a Gypsy lady beside a campfire in Dorset. It was beautifully rendered without any musical accompaniment and told the story of how she goes hawking with her big calling basket. Traditional songs are sung by the men, one being 'A Jolly Fellow'. I first heard this song whilst sheltering in a wagon during a thunderstorm:

> *Now I have dogs and ferrets too*
> *And I have them for my keeping,*
> *For I go out at the hour of night*
> *When the gamekeeper is a sleeping.*
>
> *O' I caught that hare and another one too*
> *And I put them in my pocket,*
> *I said to my dog it's time to go*
> *For the gamekeeper do ramble.*
>
> *I made my way only known to me*
> *Through the bushes and the bramble,*
> *I caught my hare and another one too*
> *And put them in my pocket.*
>
> *There's an old ale house in the valley below*
> *Down across the meadow,*
> *I'll sell that hare and the other one too*
> *Don't you think I'm a jolly fellow.*

Yes there's an old ale house in the valley below
Where the ale flows pure and yellow,
I'll give drink all around and another one too
Don't you think I'm a jolly fellow.

After the singing comes the story telling. My favourite camp-fire story is one which I heard not around the usual outside camp-fire but inside a small square tent which was heated by a wood-burning stove such as the one used in the vans.

It was a few days before Christmas and bitterly cold. A piercing wind blew along the drove but inside the little tent was cosy as we sat around the stove drinking mugs of tea whilst listening to the Gypsy man telling his stories. The first was an old Romany story which had been related to him many years ago by his wife's uncle who was then nearly a hundred.

It must first be said that the Romany is always kind and generous to tinkers, beggars and tramps or anyone less well off than himself for fear that they have been sent from above to test them. It was with this belief that the following event took place:

'A Gypsy family had fallen by hard times and feeding their two children became very difficult. One day whilst the Gypsy man was out looking for work his poor wife at home was nearly at her wits end trying to pacify her starving children. Then she had an idea as to how to obtain a little peace and told them she would boil some potatoes whereupon, unobserved by the children, she picked up a handful of pebbles and put them into the saucepan over the fire. The children anticipating the cooked potatoes quietly watched the boiling pot.

During this time a beggar came by and asked for food. The woman said she had only a crust of bread which she was saving for her husband but he was welcome to half of it. The beggar caught sight of the boiling pot and asked what was cooking in it. The Gypsy woman turned her head and whispered, so as the children would not hear, that there were only pebbles in it.

The visitor then told her to look inside the pot, and, to her amazement, when she lifted the lid she found that it was full of real food. His parting words were that the family would never go hungry again, and they never did.'

After several minutes of meditation and gazing into the fire the Gypsy man began again, with the following story:

'It so happened that a Romany man and his son were in Jerusalem on the day that Jesus Christ was crucified. They came upon a large crowd heading out of the town, and not knowing what was going on they decided to follow. When they reached a place called Calvary father and son pushed their way through the crowd to the front. Here they saw a man laid on a wooden cross and soldiers about to crucify him. On the ground close to where they were standing the large iron nails lay ready to secure the mans hands and feet. In a fit of compassion, although he did not know it was Jesus on the cross, the Romany boy asked his father,

"Shall I *chor* [steal] the nails and run?"

"Yes my son," said the Gypsy man, "Quick".

Although the boy acted immediately he managed to grab only one nail before the centurions spotted him.

Legend has it that for this action and although the attempt to save Jesus was unsuccessful the good Lord decreed that a true Romany would never be accused of stealing.'

Prophecy, Charms and Superstitions

IT IS WELL KNOWN THAT the Gypsy women are great fortune-tellers, and have been so since their history began. As early as the fifteenth century they were practising their skills as they travelled across France and Germany.

In Romany the word for fortune-telling is *dukkering*. It is derived from a mid-European word signifying something spiritual or ghostly.

It is often mistakenly believed that all Gypsies have the gift of seeing into the future, but this special power is possessed only by certain families, when it is usually inherited. But the Gypsy women who do not possess occult power, have acquired by observation the art of reading the character of the human face. Even the hands reveal a great deal to the Gypsy, not by reading the palms, but whether they are rough or smooth, a sure give away as to the occupation of their owners.

Although there are those Gypsy women who will accost one in a busy street or market with the 'cross my hand with silver lady' and then gaze at your palm and tell you that you are about to receive a sum of money, there are also families who consider it dangerous to dabble with the unknown and do not partake in any form of *dukkering*, or fortune-telling. On the other hand the

Lee family are particularly well known for their inherited gift of prophecy. Every summer on Weymouth promenade the bow-top van of Gypsy Lee can be seen. She is a descendant of Gypsy Petulengro Lee the famous *dukkerer* and if you wish to know what the future holds for you, for a small fee she will tell you.

I have encountered three Gypsy women with the gift of prophecy. Eiza Cooper who was a regular caller to my house collecting rags, related many stories about her past whilst drinking her tea. She came she said from the Black Coopers, and was known as Black Liz. The term, black blood (*kaulo ratti*), means the purest type of Romany. The Black Coopers possessed the gift of prophecy and Eiza's husband had foreseen his own death when he was in perfect health. He told her how one night he awoke to see an angel sitting at the end of his bed beckoning to him. A short time after he died.

Another member of the Cooper family who was camped high on the downs above Salisbury was Granny Caroline Cooper. She also inherited the Black Coopers' gift of prophecy.

One day when she was out calling at a village in the valley, selling things from her big basket, she was asked to read the hand of a farm worker. She predicted that he would soon be rich enough not to have to work again. A short time after this the man was ploughing a field when one of the blades struck an object. He went back to see the cause of the obstruction and was amazed to find a pot in the furrow with its contents of gold coins scattered over the ground. This eventually led to the farm worker gaining a small fortune and not having to work again. According to Eiza, Granny Cooper was also well rewarded for her prediction.

The following happened quite recently when a Romany

lady also a descendant of the New Forest Coopers, predicted that her pregnant daughter-in-law would give birth to a boy even though she had been scanned and told she was expecting a girl. Unlike in former days, when Gypsy babies were born in their camps, the expectant mothers now enjoy all the modern facilities of the nearest hospital. But when the young mother came back to the camp she was not holding in her arms a baby girl as the modern technology had indicated but a boy just as the Romany grandmother had foreseen.

Gypsy mother showing off her new baby, Dorset.

Something very similar happened to a member of my family when she was expecting her second child. She was visited by a Gypsy lady who told her that the child she was carrying would be a boy to which my cousin replied that as she already had a son she felt this was going to be a girl. However the Gypsy was adamant that it would be a boy, and an easy birth, as she would be with her in spirit. On repeating this to her gynaecologist he said "surely you don't believe all that!" But when the baby was born and she was handed her son the doctor said "well the gypsy was with you after all". The birth also was incredibly easy.

On calling again to see my cousin the Gypsy said she felt the presence of her parents. They had been visiting her that morning but had left just before the Gypsy came. There was she said an evil eye on the house; at that time the neighbours were being troublesome.

The Gypsy then went on to say that there is happiness now but there will also be great sadness. It was not long after that my cousin's husband died suddenly. A little while after his death the Gypsy called again. Feeling that she could not face her my cousin sent her mother to the door but the Gypsy insisted that she speak to the lady of the house. On seeing my cousin the Romany lady took her hand and said that she knew that her husband had died, and went on to say,

"It was the water wasn't it?"

To which my cousin replied, "No he had a heart attack."

"Yes," replied the Gypsy, "but it was the water; you think about it."

Although slightly bewildered my cousin was comforted by the Gypsy woman's visit. Later that day the meaning of the Gypsy's words suddenly became clear. A few months before her husband's death they had been on holiday in Wales when someone got into difficulties whilst swimming. Her husband immediately swam to the rescue but it was a long way out and when he eventually returned to shore he was exhausted. After this he was never really fit again. That was probably what the Gypsy was referring to. I find this a remarkable story and it helped my cousin through a very sad time.

In the mind of the *gorgio* the dusky people of the Romany race are all possessed with magical powers, both of prophecy and healing, and for this reason tend to hold them in awe. Although this not entirely true it must be recognized that there are certain Gypsy women (it is nearly always the women) who have knowledge of the medicinal properties of certain herbs who have performed incredible feats of healing, either by the use of herbal medicines or, even more remarkably, by charms.

Romany lady driving a flat cart, Wiltshire.

There have been many accounts of warts being charmed away, each Gypsy woman having her own magical method of achieving it. A Wiltshire Romany recommends impaling a piece of meat on the sharp thorn of a blackthorn bush; as the meat rots the warts will shrivel, and as the meat drops from the bush so the wart will fall off. A similar cure is given by a New Forest Romany only this time using a large black slug instead of meat. I have heard said that an old Gypsy woman who travelled in Hampshire could charm away warts just by looking at them.

Then there are those charms which are believed to keep away illness, most of which are based on herbal content. Burdock seed in a little bag worn around the neck is said to prevent rheumatism. The New Forest Romanies carry a sprig of gorse in the pocket to keep away fever. Sprays of rosemary hanging in a Romany tent or van will give protection against all things evil.

There is a lovely story told by a forester neighbour of mine as to how a small ivory miniature of a white hare was found in an old Romany van on the hill opposite my cottage. As hares are the animals above all others associated with magic, particularly the white hare, then this ivory miniature must have been the lucky charm of the Gypsy who once lived in the van.

A charm which was worn only by the New Forest Gypsies was a ring made from plaited horse hair. Eiza Cooper told a fascinating story as to how she would spend hours trying to approach the wild ponies close enough to pull strands of hair from their manes and tails. But the ponies had to be either skewbald or piebald, as rings made from the hair of ponies this colour were believed to bring good luck to the wearer. The Spanish Gypsies used cord braided from the hair of a black mare's tail to thread their charms on. The charms were in the form of small horns with silver tips. These worn around the neck were thought to ward off the evil eye. The evil eye, according to the superstition, is casting an evil look at people who afterwards fall sick.

Charms and superstitions are very much connected.

It is often said that the Gypsy has no superstitions but did not the origin of their greatest tradition, that of burning the vans after the owner's death, originate from their great fear of the spirits of the dead. It must be said, however, that the practice of burning the van of the deceased is no longer carried out, probably for economic reasons. It is believed by many Gypsies that to carry a piece of bread in their pockets will give them protection against ghosts and evil spirits.

A superstition which I share with the Romanies is that of not bringing snowdrops into the house. I love to see these flowers growing and make pilgrimages every year to a certain stream where the banks are covered with drifts of this pure white flower. To me they hold the promise of spring. I once gathered a bunch and placed them in a vase indoors; the next day I heard of my grandmother's death. Although the Gypsies gather snowdrops from the woods and bunch them up to sell from their big baskets, they never have them inside their vans or tents.

Another plant which the Gypsies believe to be extremely unlucky is the wild thyme. This is a plant I associate very much with the downland, it is strongly aromatic and attracts a profusion of bees and butterflies. Unlike the Gypsies I gather bunches of this when the little mauve flowers are out. Hung upside down they dry out and keep their colour all through the winter.

The following is not a superstition of bad luck or evil spirits but a belief. Juliette de Bairacli-Levy writes in her book *Wanderers in the New Forest*:

'The coming of the frog into the well tub gave much pleasure to my children. For my part, whenever I met the frog I thought of the Gypsy belief that water in which a frog will dwell is always pure enough for humans to drink. The belief has origin in an old legend concerning the Holy Mary and a frog. To quote:

After Christ was crucified, Mary, back from the cross and weeping, met with a female frog who said to her:

'Weep not, good woman.'

'How can I not weep when they have crucified my son!'

'Alas, poor woman! I had twelve children. They lay in a wheel rut. A wagon came along and all twelve were killed. I do not weep over twelve but accept my destiny. Why then dost thou weep for one?'

Mary, consoled, then gave this answer:

'O frog! Blessed shalt thou be for ever. Wherever thou art, water shall always be clear, and mankind will drink it with pleasure.'

Romany Recipes

THE ROMANY DIET IS MUCH healthier than that of the *gorgio* for he rarely eats convenience foods. His main meal is invariably cooked over the fire in a big stew-pot, and apart from the meat there will be a variety of natural ingredients included such as vegetables, mushrooms and wild herbs freshly gathered. These days the meat will usually be purchased from the butcher, but at one time the Romany was a skilled poacher – pheasant, rabbit and hare were regularly eaten.

The methods used to acquire the game were all carried out quickly and silently. Nothing was poached which was not needed for the pot. Killing for sport is not in the Gypsy's nature. His hunting possessions were simple – just a catapult, nets, a couple of ferrets and sometimes a dog. I recall being shown one of their sturdy catapults by a flamboyantly dressed Gypsy man whilst walking with him along a drove on the Hampshire downs. He was boasting of his ability to be able to bring down a roosting pheasant with it. I enjoyed much more holding one of the ferrets belonging to another Romany. I was agreeably surprised to find that it was not ferocious and did not attempt to bite even though I held it tighter than necessary; it was so mobile I thought I would lose it. When the Gypsy man took it from me he just let it slip smoothly through one hand to the other.

The ferrets were put down the rabbit holes after all

the exits had been covered by nets. The rabbits bolting from the ferrets would go straight into the nets, where the Gypsy would be waiting. Sometimes little muzzles were put on the ferrets to stop them killing a rabbit and eating it underground, known as 'laying up'. But the Romany feeds his ferrets well and has no need to do this, but it will instinctively hunt.

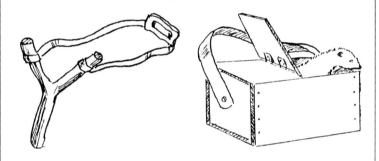

Poaching of another sort took place up on the downs. On moonlit nights the hare becomes easy prey to any cunning, stealthy poacher. The hare is a handsome animal – tawny grey, with a tinge of rufous. It does not burrow in the ground but squats in a hidden spot known as a form. By night it comes out to feed on its favourite diet of clover, grass, turnips and corn; it will also nibble the bark of young trees.

By the light of the moon the poacher approaches the hare from a distance, whereupon the animal would immediately squat and flatten its ears, believing itself to be hidden. The poacher then puts a stick into the ground and hangs his coat upon it leaving the hare with its eyes fixed upon the coat. In the meantime the poacher has quietly retreated and moved in a wide circle to silently approach the animal from the rear. The hare, being so intent with the danger seemingly at his front is seized from behind – a form of poaching which takes patience and lightness of foot.

Gypsy boys seem to be attracted more to the streams and rivers to try their skills in catching something for the pot. I recollect a young Gypsy boy who many years ago was camped with his family in one of the chalk hollows at Odstock. Often he would come down to the neighbouring village of Britford where there were several small chalk streams. These were tributaries of the Avon and one in particular, which had a very stony bed, was well known for its cray-fish. It was here that the village children, myself included, fished for minnows with a jam jar. The Gypsy boy always paddled the stream with a net held down-current, then turned over the stones hoping a crayfish would shoot straight into it which sometimes it did. Another method he used was to try and entice the crayfish into the net by baiting it with a piece of meat, of which they are particularly fond. He occasionally caught enough for a meal to take back to his camp.

At other times the Gypsy boy would find his way across the meadow to a trout stream, and with a wary eye for the water bailiff, try his luck at 'tickling' a trout at which he was very skilled. The method he used was to get quietly into the stream, and then feel under the water for cavities in the bank where the fish hide up. He would then place one hand over the entrance to prevent the fish darting out. As soon as the smooth side of the fish was felt by the other hand the tips of the fingers were brought gently against the abdomen, and gradually the hand closed over the trout. The fish was then suddenly grasped, snatched out of the hole, and flung onto the bank.

Before Salisbury Plain came under the plough and dividing fences were erected it was a paradise for the Gypsies. They could drive their horse-drawn wagons across the sheep-cropped turf and camp for the night in the shelter of the droves. It was from the hedges along these tracks that they gathered fruits to make their jams and cordials, blackberries, wild raspberries, and sloes. Although the Gypsies were not great cooks, for their meals were usually cooked outdoors in a big stew-pot over a camp-fire, they did make use of the berries. The patience taken by these folk to pick sufficient tiny wild raspberries to make even one pot of jam was to be admired. When my mother was living on the downs Granny Sheen told her how she made her jam.

Granny Sheen's Wild Raspberry Jam

Hull the berries, allow one pound of sugar to one pound of berries. Put layers of berries and sugar alternately in a pan to the depth of four inches. Leave for two hours, very gently bring to the boil, simmer till fruit is tender. Skim as soon as boiling point if reached. Do not stir while cooking. Pour into dishes, not allowing preserve to be more than three inches deep. Stand outside in the hot sun for a day or two, bringing indoors at night. At the end of two days the preserve should be jellied and the fruit be firm and plump ready to pot up.

ea

The Romany diet varied slightly according to the area in which they were travelling. Squirrels would probably have been added to the stew-pot of the New Forest Gypsies along with rabbit, whereas in the Wiltshire countryside they had an abundant supply of their favourite delicacy the hedgehog. Hare and pheasant too would certainly have been in the pot for the evening meal.

Hotchi-Witchi (Hedgehog)

There are two ways of cooking hedgehog but the location of the Romany camp determines which it shall be. One method is to enclose it in clay and bake it in the glowing embers of the fire. When cooked the clay is removed together with the spines leaving the meat ready to eat. This way though can only be enjoyed by travellers where the soil is of clay. As the downland is a very chalky soil the Romany there has to cook his *hotchi-witchi* over the fire on a spit.

ea

Another favourite delicacy of the Gypsies was the edible snails (*bowie*) that were so plentiful on the chalk downs. The large type with a brown and white stripe shell was a particular favourite. To kill the snails they were dropped into boiling water, a quick and instantaneous way. They were hooked out of their shells with a thorn, washed thoroughly and made into a soup.

Snails are best for eating if gathered after a frost. They are no good at all in summer:

Bowie Zoomi (Snail Soup)

The snails are cooked in water with a mixture of wild herbs for two or three hours, until they were tender. The soup is then eaten with bread and butter. Sometimes the snails are picked out from the soup dipped in salt and eaten separately.

🌣

Boiled savoury pudding is a traditional meal which is still cooked and enjoyed by travelling families to this day:

Savoury Pudding

Cut into thin slices pieces of cooked meat and bacon. Peel an onion and some apples, and cut them into slices. Make a stiff dough with flour and water, roll it out thinly:

first lay the slices of meat and bacon on this to cover, and over the meat and bacon place the slices of onion and apple, and then sprinkle with sage; roll up the paste to encase the ingredients. Place the long pudding in a cloth, tie each end and put in a large pot over the fire with plenty of water and boil for two hours.

⋆

The Romany has a very good way to stop the pudding from sticking to the pot, and and that is to put spoons and forks in the bottom first.

Any cold left-overs are fried later.

The way the Romany does his frying is to put the bacon or meat in the pan over the fire for a minute or two to melt the fat, then the rest of the ingredients are added with just enough water to cover.

⋆

The following recipe was told to me by a New Forest Gypsy many years ago. For generations the Forest Gypsies have made a home-brew with the leaves of the aromatic bog myrtle, or sweet gale as it is sometimes called.

Bog Myrtle Beer

Gather enough bog myrtle leaves to fill a container, taking care to pick only the leaves, and press down. Make a syrup of boiling water and honey, allowing a pound of honey to a gallon of water, providing enough syrup to cover the leaves. Leave to cool and then add an ounce of dry yeast. Cover and leave to stand for twenty-four hours, then strain liquor into cask. At the end of a week bottle off and cork down firmly.

Herb Beer (Gypsy Petulengro)

Two ounces of burdock leaves, one ounce yarrow, one ounce dandelion herb, eight ounces malt, one ounce hops, two ounces sugar, one ounce yeast.

Place all but the sugar and yeast in a large pan with ten pints of water. Boil for two hours (gently simmering after it has once boiled). Strain off the liquor into an earthenware pan if possible (if not, an enamelled pan.) When the liquor is just 'blood warm', stir in the sugar and yeast. Let it stand in a warm place for twenty-four hours. Place a piece of cloth over the pan during this time. After that time has elapsed, skim off the yeast that has risen to the top and bottle the liquor (in screw-top bottles for preference), putting the corks 'lightly' into the bottles at first. Twelve hours later tighten them up. Stand away for a day or two, and the brew will be ready to drink. N.B. It is advisable to mix the yeast and the sugar together before pouring into the bulk of the brew, using a little of the cooled liquor to mix them with.

Tonic Stout (Gypsy Petulengro)

One ounce of nettles, one ounce hops, eight ounces black (or burnt) malt, quarter once liquorice, two medium sized potatoes, two ounces brown sugar, one ounce yeast.

First add the herbs, malt, and hops to ten pints of water. Boil up and add the liquor and the potatoes. The latter should be washed well but not peeled, and should be perforated with a fork or darning needle. Gently simmer until you have about eight pints of the liquor left. Turn out into an earthenware pan if possible, after straining, and then stir in the yeast and sugar, which should have been mixed beforehand with a little of the liquor cooled in a cup or jug. Stir well into the liquor. Stand in a warm place for twenty-four hours and bottle in exactly the same manner as described in the Herb Beer recipe. If you want the 'ruby' tint, add an apple and a few rusty nails for the 'iron'.

Leave for a couple of days after corking and watch the beautiful creamy stout when poured out.

Do not shake the bottle when uncorking.

☙

The Gypsies also drank herb-teas as well as strong ordinary tea, especially the older generation who had a deep knowledge of the medicinal value of herbs. The droves and hedgerows contain a wealth of herbs and these were readily gathered by the Gypsies. Some they used fresh whilst others they dried for use during the winter. Wild raspberry canes grew in profusion along the droves. As well as supplying the travelling folk with sweet fruit their leaves made a refreshing medicinal tea.

Raspberry Leaf Tea

Take a handful of dried raspberry leaves, put them in a pot, pour boiling water over them, and leave to infuse. Strain and sweeten with honey.

A favourite brew of the Sheen family from Hindon was made from a mixture of downland herbs and flowers.

Downland Tea

Take a handful of leaves of the wild raspberry, wild strawberry, blackberry, thyme and cowslip flower heads. Dry and mix together well. Use two teaspoons to a cup of water. Sweeten with honey.

A group of travellers on the road in Dorset.

Romany Remedies

LIVING AS THEY DID, CONSTANTLY travelling from one remote place to another, the Gypsies were unable to visit or call the *Mulahl-Moosh-Engro* (Doctor) if they were not well. With the healthy outdoor life they lived they were seldom ill but there were minor ailments to contend with such as cuts and bruises, colds and coughs. To deal with these when they occurred they had their own remedies, embrocations, ointments, cough mixtures and liniments, mainly prepared from herbs and plants.

The Gypsies of the Wiltshire countryside were fortunate in having at their disposal the herb they prized above all – the elder. Their respect for this tree was so great they would never burn its wood on their fires. This prolific tree of the chalk soil provided the Gypsies with its medicinal properties through its blossom, leaves, berries and bark.

I remember as a child being confined to bed with a heavy cold when a Gypsy lady came hawking at the door. On hearing of my plight she told my mother of a soothing remedy using elderberries.

Elder Syrup – For a Cold

Place two quarts of elderberries into a stone jar, and cover with a plate. Place the jar in a pan of boiling water until the juice flows. Turn the berries into a sieve with a piece of muslin in it, gather the ends of the muslin together and squeeze the berries. Put the juice in a pan with one pound of sugar to each quart of juice, add a few cloves and bring to the boil. When cold, strain, put into small bottles, cork and keep in a cool place.

Blackberry Drink – Also for a Cold

Three pounds of blackberries, one pint of vinegar. Put together and allow to soak for twenty-four hours, strain and add one pound of sugar and to every pint of juice; add six cloves and one ounce of root ginger; boil together for half an hour. Strain, then bottle.

Sloe Syrup – For a Sore Throat

Gather ripe sloes free from stalks and leaves, and put them in layers, alternate with sugar, in wide-mouthed jars. Put in a good layer of sloes, then a couple of tablespoonfuls of sugar, and keep on till the jars are full.

Cork down and put away for three or four weeks till the sloes have shrivelled and sunk to the bottom. Drain off the syrup and cork down.

Elder Ointment – For Bruises

Pick the blossom of the elder when the sun is full on them. Crush them slightly. Get some pig's fat, before the butcher adds salt to it, and boil it down. Add the crushed elder. Leave to cool, and pot up.

Elder Oil – For Minor Burns and Scalds

Pick elder flower in full bloom. Put in a wide-top jar and

tie down. Place in the sun. Keep jar re-filled to replace shrinkage. When all the oil has oozed out strain into a bottle. It will keep indefinitely. Rub gently on effected part, it will sting, but heals well.

☙

Another plant that was once loved by travellers as well as the Romanies was the wild clematis or, as it is so appropriately called, traveller's joy. It grows and en-twines every hedgerow on the chalk soil of Wiltshire. In the days when the only means of travel across the Plain was on foot, by donkey cart or horse-drawn vehicles, the traveller became dusty and weary. The leaves and flowers of traveller's joy provided these people with many of their needs – cool leaves to place on sun-burn, a refreshing tea to revive the spirit or a brew when cold to wash away the dust from the eyes. In the autumn, when the flowers of traveller's joy have turned to fluffy seed, it becomes known as 'old mans beard'.

Wild Clematis Tea

A small handful of dried leaves and flowers to a cup of boiling water; leave to infuse for two or three minutes; sweeten with honey.

For Lumbago

In the days when juniper bushes were to be found easily on the plain the Gypsies gathered the berries and pounded them to extract the oil. A little of this oil was used to run on the effected spot.

☙

There is one old remedy, 'Romany Balm', which must be included in this short collection. As Gypsy Petulengro said in his book – *Romany Remedies and Recipes* – it is as old as the hills and scarcely ever fails to effect a cure of skin complaints."

Balm ('Romany Balm'): Gypsy Petulengro

Four ounces of the fat from the kidney of the pig, one ounce of cuttings from the 'Frog of the horse hoof'*, one house leek (the plant that grows on the tiles of cottages), one ounce scrapings of the bark of the elder tree.

Place altogether in an enamelled pan over a slow heat. Stir while the fat is 'sizzling', then strain off (after half an hour's simmering) into a clean jar and use on any sores, skin-complaints, cuts, boils, bruises, etc.

Gypsy Foot Ointment (Gypsy Petulengro)

Four ounces tallow, one ounce powdered sulphur, one ounce olive oil.

Melt together and stir well while it is cooling. Rub a little on the feet before a walk. No corns will ever appear if you use this.

Rheumatism and Arthritis

Stew a few sticks of celery in a small amount of milk or water, and eat juice and all. Do this for a week.

☙

The following remedy was told to me by a lady from Tollard Royal in Wiltshire. For years she had been suffering from a painful swollen elbow which doctors

---

*The horse-hoof clippings can be obtained from any farrier, who usually throws them away.

said they could do nothing for. The remedy had been recommended to her by a Gypsy, and when applied to her swollen elbow it cured it.

To Cure Any Painful Swelling

Collect some worms and put into an old medicine bottle. Bury the bottle containing the worms in a hot manure heap and leave for some months. When the bottle is taken out of the manure heap the worms will have shrunk and shrivelled into the bottom of the bottle, but a clear golden oil will have replaced them. This oil if applied to the affected part is said to cure any painful swelling.

Deafness (Gypsy Petulengro)

Melt the fat from the *Hotchi–witchi* (hedgehog) and drop into the ear at night. This relieves the ear-drum and dissolves the hard wax which is the frequent cause of deafness. This is a fine old Gypsy remedy. A good substitute for the hedgehog fat is the fat of the ordinary goose. Melt a little of this a drop little of it, warm, in the ear when in bed, and sleep lying on the opposite ear. Next night do the other ear.

For Earache

When paunching a hedgehog a bright blue-green bag will be found. This bag contains an oil which is very good for the treatment of earache.

Also For Earache

Make a little ball of salt by tying it inside a piece of muslin; warm over the fire and lay on it.

Blood-Pressure

Boil one ounce of the common stinging nettle in one pint of water for five minutes. Strain and re-boil the liquid before bottling. Take a small wine glass three times daily.

❧

Travellers of today have a great knowledge of the medicinal properties of the herbs of the countryside and still make good use of them. Plantain leaves are particularly popular with them.

For wounds, bites and stings

Plantain is a powerful herb, and the leaves applied to the sting of a nettle is even more effective in treating it than that of the dock. The smooth side of the leaves on a wound are used for drawing out an infection and the rough side for healing.

Heartburn

The Romany has a very simple remedy for heartburn; he simply takes a piece of charcoal from his camp-fire and chews it.

Chamomile Tea – To Calm the Nerves

Put about thirty flowers into a jug, on to these pour a

pint of boiling water, cover and leave to stand for fifteen minutes, strain into another jug; sweeten with a little honey. A little grated ginger may be added if liked.

Elder Blossom – Treatment of the Eyes

The following is a moving story of a travelling Gypsy herbalist who met a soldier who had been blinded at Dunkirk. A travelling Gypsy woman saw a blind soldier and noted his sadness; she advised the use of elder blossom as a treatment for the eyes. The soldier's father carefully applied the treatment; the elder blossom began to cause pain in the soldier's eyes, and the family lost faith and stopped the treatment. But on a further visit the Gypsy met the soldier again and saw that his eyes had improved. She persuaded the family to continue with the elder blossom, and the final result was that full sight was restored to the soldier's eyes. (One day in his world of darkness, he saw a glimmer. It was his mother's wedding ring. Slowly the power of sight returned to the blind eyes.)

A Herbal Tobacco (Juliette de Bairacli-Levy)

To a base of dried, finely rubbed coltsfoot leaves, add in smaller proportion (blending to individual taste), thyme, rosemary, eye-bright, ground-ivy and wood-betony, lily-of-the-valley leaves (all or any, as available). All dried and finely sifted. Smoke in a clay pipe.

Puffball (Fungi): Juliette de Bairacli-Levy

When crushed and applied to wounds will check excessive bleeding and promote healing. Learnt from the

Manouche Gypsies of Alsace-Lorraine.

Sphagnum Moss: Juliette de Bairacli-Levy

Sphagnum moss, partly dried and then soaked in a brew of a strongly antiseptic herb such as garlic, elder blossom, wormwood, rue, etc., is much used by Gypsies for skin and wound treatments.

Bolting Rabbits From Their Holes

Get some coarse brown paper and cut it into strips about eighteen inches long and two inches wide. Make a solution of the following: four ounces Saltpetre, half ounce Cayenne Pepper, enough vinegar to make a 'pasty' solution.

Brush over the paper with this solution and then roll the paper into loose rolls. Dry them well before using.

Now place one of the rolls of paper into the hole on the windward side, light it up, and lay a piece of turf over the hole when it is well alight. Watch the other holes or place nets over them.

Herbal Treatment For Horses

With so much depending on his horse the Romany man has naturally become an expert in its welfare. He usually has a remedy for any ailment the animal might suffer. Their decoctions contain mostly herbs, berries, and bark gathered from the hedgerows. Mixed with other ingredients such as oats and black treacle they prove just as effective as a medicine prescribed by a veterinary surgeon.

Into the Sunset

THE FUTURE OF THE GENUINE Gypsy traveller in this country has never looked more precarious. Nomadic tribes have been persecuted for centuries throughout Asia and Europe but have survived mainly due to their ability to endure and to the large areas of land through which they were able to move. Not wanted in one place there was always somewhere a bit further on where they could find a place to rest their vans and pitch their tents.

That degree of space does not exist in this small island of ours. There are ever decreasing areas of common land or ancient droves where Gypsies can practice their traditional way of life. Land hungry owners have been pushing out their boundaries, clearing land which for centuries has been used by all. With the advent of the New Age traveller and the troubles that followed in their wake through illegal gatherings, every attempt has been made to deny them space.

Laws have been passed and others are being considered to prevent the nuisance being caused by the gatherings of hundreds of these so-called travellers. The arrival of convoys of old buses and vans encroaching on habited areas has created an atmosphere of hate against all forms of travellers. Consequently and inevitably the restrictions are making life very difficult for the genuine long term traveller.

And so the true Gypsy families, like my friends along

the drove, feel themselves increasingly hemmed in. Their survival depends on fodder for their horses, without which they cannot continue their nomadic existence. They are obliged to travel from one camping site to another as the available grass is eaten by their horses.

A group of Romany vans parked in an old drove is pleasing to most people and indicates a link with the past. They leave no rubbish, the only evidence that they have been at any particular spot is the remains of their fire and gentle cropping of the surrounding grass. I could not begin to describe the delight which I felt when I first found the family on the drove or the precious hours I have spent with them. Are we to lose all this?

It is certainly going to require much thought and diplomacy to arrive at a solution in the future. Great moves were made to build sites and permanently house Gypsies but to those who know nothing else but the open road this is akin to imprisonment. It will need the wisdom of Solomon to decide which of the travellers on the road today are the true Gypsy race that history has handed down and which are the drop-outs trying to act like them.

For years fruit farms and vegetable farms have enjoyed the enthusiastic and hard working help from their Gypsy visitors. They would be sadly missed should they disappear altogether.

I sincerely hope that this unique race of people will survive and that the love of the British people for tradition will come to their aid.

This is summed up by Robert Louis Stevenson who said, "There is nobody under thirty so dead but his heart will stir a little at sight of a gypsies' camp."

CONTENTMENT

A gypsy told me where to see
The orchid scented sweet and rare;
On downland side with cowslip fair,
A feast for butterfly and bee.

A gypsy told me where there'd be
Wild raspberries juicy red and sweet;
In hedgerows warmed by summer heat,
Midst fragrant flowers and grassy sea.

A gypsy told me of a place
Where glow-worms shine as darkness falls,
On banks of drove as first owl calls
And moths take flight on wings of lace.

A gypsy told me where to find
The greatest treasure of them all;
Where flowers bloom and wild birds call,
Contentment joy and peace of mind.

Irene Soper

If you have enjoyed reading The Romany Way, *you may like to see some other books published by Ex Libris Press in our Country Bookshelf series. These are as follows:*

LETTERS FROM THE ENGLISH COUNTRYSIDE
Essays on rural topics from a master of the genre
by Ralph Whitlock; £4.95

THE SECRET LANE
A country story
by Ralph Whitlock; £4.95

MARCH WINDS & APRIL SHOWERS:
Country weather lore
by Ralph Whitlock; £3.50

O WHO WILL MARRY ME?
A Book of Country Love
by Ralph Whitlock; £3.50

LAND GIRL
Her story of six years in the Women's Land Army
by Anne Hall; £4.95

LUMBER JILL
Her story of four years in the Women's Timber Corps
by Mavis Williams; £3.95

VILLAGE PRACTICE
A year in the life of a country doctor's wife
by Anne Stratford; £4.95

CHRISTIANA AWDRY'S HOUSEHOLD BOOK
Eighteenth century recipes and household tips
by Margaret Jensen; £4.95

GRAN'S OLD-FASHIONED REMEDIES, WRINKLES & RECIPES
by Jean Penny; £3.50

GRAN'S OLD-FASHIONED GARDENING GEMS
by Jean Penny; £3.50

BELT & BUCKLE
An hilarious tale of a 1950s boyhood
by Toby Dyer; £4.95

MAISIE & ME
A country childhood in the 1920s
by Stella Ashton; £3.95

WINIFRED:
Her Childhood and early Working Life
by Sylvia Marlow; £4.50

Ex Libris Press books may be obtained through your local bookshop or direct from the publisher, post-free, at

1 The Shambles, Bradford on Avon, Wiltshire, BA15 1JS

Tel/Fax 01225 863595

In addition to the above books, Ex Libris Press also publishes books on the West Country and the Channel Islands. Please ask for our free, illustrated list.